P9-CQK-979

AMERICAN
WAR LIBRARY

★ ★ ★ ★

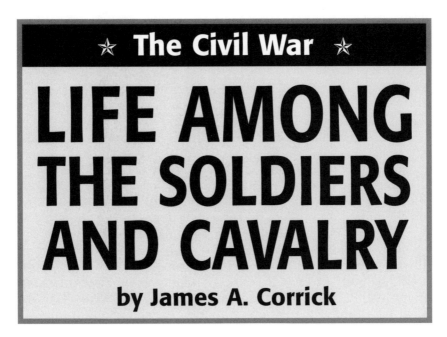

★ The Civil War ★

LIFE AMONG THE SOLDIERS AND CAVALRY

by James A. Corrick

Lucent Books, P.O. Box 289011, San Diego, CA 92198-9011

Titles in The American War Library series include:

World War II
Hitler and the Nazis
Kamikazes
Leaders and Generals
Life as a POW
Life of an American Soldier in
  Europe
Strategic Battles in Europe
Strategic Battles in the Pacific
The War at Home
Weapons of War

The Civil War
Leaders of the North and South
Life Among the Soldiers and
  Cavalry
Lincoln and the Abolition of
  Slavery
Strategic Battles
Weapons of War

For Rachel, who always brings sparkle into our lives

Library of Congress Cataloging-in-Publication Data

Corrick, James A.
  Life among the soldiers and cavalry / by James A. Corrick.
   p. cm.—(American war library series)
  Includes bibliographical references and index.
  Summary: Discusses life among Civil War soldiers and cavalry
including joining up, uniform and rifles, training and discipline,
on the march, in battle, and returning home.
  ISBN 1-56006-491-9 (lib. bdg. : alk. paper)
  1. United States. Army—History—Civil War, 1861–1865
Juvenile literature. 2. United States. Army—Military Life—History
—19th century Juvenile literature. 3. Confederate States of America.
Army—Military life Juvenile literature. 4. United States—History—
Civil War, 1861–1865—Cavalry operations Juvenile literature.
5. Soldiers—United States—History—19th century—Juvenile
literature. 6. Soldiers—Confederate States of America Juvenile
literature. I. Title. II. Series.
E607.C67 2000
973.7'42—dc21
                      99-28237
                        CIP

★ Contents ★

A Nation Forged by War

The United States, like many nations, was forged and defined by war. Despite Benjamin Franklin's opinion that "There never was a good war or a bad peace," the United States owes its very existence to the War of Independence, one to which Franklin wholeheartedly subscribed. The country forged by war in 1776 was tempered and made stronger by the Civil War in the 1860s.

The Texas Revolution, the Mexican-American War, and the Spanish-American War expanded the country's borders and gave it overseas possessions. These wars made the United States a world power, but this status came with a price, as the nation became a key but reluctant player in both World War I and World War II.

Each successive war further defined the country's role on the world stage. Following World War II, U.S. foreign policy redefined itself to focus on the role of defender, not only of the freedom of its own citizens, but also of the freedom of people everywhere. During the cold war that followed World War II until the collapse of the Soviet Union, defending the world meant fighting communism. This goal, manifested in the Korean and Vietnam conflicts, proved elusive, and soured the American public on its achievability. As the United States emerged as the world's sole superpower, American foreign policy has been guided less by national interest and more on protecting international human rights. But as involvement in Somalia and Kosovo prove, this goal has been equally elusive.

As a result, the country's view of itself changed. Bolstered by victories in World Wars I and II, Americans first relished the role of protector. But, as war followed war in a seemingly endless procession, Americans began to doubt their leaders, their motives, and themselves. The Vietnam War especially caused people to question the validity of sending its young people to die in places where they were not particularly wanted and for people who did not seem especially grateful.

While the most obvious changes brought about by America's wars have been geopolitical in nature, many other aspects of society have been touched. War often does not bring about change directly, but acts instead like the catalyst in a chemical reaction, accelerating changes already in progress.

Some of these changes have been societal. The role of women in the United States had been slowly changing, but World War II put thousands into the workforce and into uniform. They might have gone back to being housewives after the war, but equality, once experienced, would not be forgotten.

Likewise, wars have accelerated technological change. The necessity for faster airplanes and a more destructive bomb led to the development of jet planes and nuclear energy. Artificial fibers developed for parachutes in the 1940s were used in the clothing of the 1950s.

Lucent Books' American War Library covers key wars in the development of the nation. Each war is covered in several volumes, to allow for more detail, context, and to provide volumes on often neglected subjects, such as the kamikazes of World War II, or weapons used in the Civil War. As with all Lucent Books, notes, annotated bibliographies, and appendixes such as glossaries give students a launching point for further research. In addition, sidebars and archival photographs enhance the text. Together, each volume in The American War Library will aid students in understanding how America's wars have shaped and changed its politics, economics, and society.

War Between the States

The American Civil War (1861–1865) was the largest and bloodiest war ever fought in the Western Hemisphere. Almost 3.5 million men served in the two armies that battled across the Southern third of the continental United States. No matter what their uniform, the soldiers and cavalry lived a life apart from the civilian populations of the North and South. Their daily lives were filled with the tedium and strain of army camp routine—chores, drill, and discipline—punctuated by brutal combat, the horrors of which were unimaginable to outsiders and which would kill six hundred thousand in four years of fighting.

North and South

The conflict that engaged these men began in 1861 when eleven Southern states—Alabama, Arkansas, Florida, Georgia, Louisiana, Mississippi, North Carolina, South Carolina, Tennessee, Texas, and Virginia—seceded from the United States to form an independent country, the Confederate States of America, also known as the Confederacy.

The issues that led to secession were many, but their roots lay in the different ways of life found in the South and the North. The South was almost entirely a farming region, with few factories. Its main crops were cotton and tobacco, which were sold not only to the Northern states but all over the world. This farming economy depended on the labor of 3.5 million African American slaves, who made up over a third of the total 9 million people living in the South.

The North, particularly along the Atlantic coast, was heavily industrialized and had a large population of 23 million. Much of the profit earned from Southern crops went to buy farm equipment, clothing, and other manufactured goods from Northern factories. As historian Samuel Carter notes:

> The North had three-quarters of the Nation's wealth; and more than five

times the manufacturing capacity of the South. . . . The North had nearly three times the railroad mileage of the South, a waterways transportation system, and a network of generally well-surfaced highways.[1]

Although prejudice against African Americans was nationwide, the institution of slavery had never developed in the North. In the decades preceding the Civil War, the differences between South and North gave rise to much political conflict. Slavery came to represent this conflict.

In the North, vocal activists known as abolitionists called for the abolishment of slavery. Southerners believed that slavery was such an important part of their society

and economy that both would be destroyed by its elimination. They also resented Northern outsiders dictating how they should and should not live.

In November 1860, Abraham Lincoln was elected president as a candidate of the abolitionist Republican Party; Southerners saw his election as the first step in a program that would ruin their Southern society. Within six weeks of the election, South Carolina became the first Southern state to secede.

To Preserve the Union

As president of the United States, or the Union, Lincoln refused to recognize the Confederacy as a separate country and declared the U.S. government ready to de-

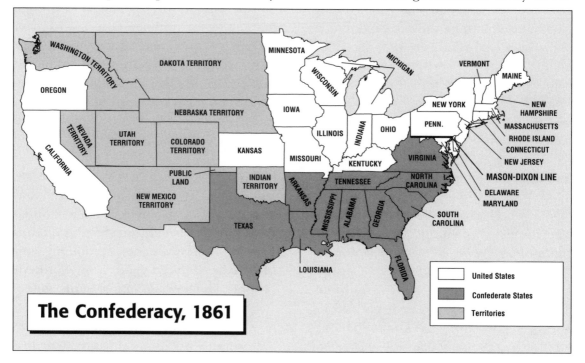

The Confederacy, 1861

United States

Confederate States

Territories

clare war to bring the Southern states back into the Union. The Confederate States were just as determined to fight for their independence. War came on April 12, 1861, when Confederate forces fired on the Union's Fort Sumter in the harbor of Charleston, South Carolina.

The Union's military strategy was threefold. In the east, the Federal army set out to capture Richmond, Virginia, the capital of the Confederacy. In the west, it was determined to take control of the Mississippi River, thus isolating the far western Confederate states from the eastern.

At sea, the Federal navy blockaded the Confederacy. Navy ships cruised the Con-

Confederate artillerymen fire on Fort Sumter on April 12, 1861. The bombardment marked the beginning of the Civil War.

federate coast and kept ships from reaching Southern ports with essential supplies of guns and other goods, which the South's few factories could produce only in limited quantities.

The Southern Strategy

The Confederacy, on the other hand, relied on a defensive strategy, its goal to wear down the North until the latter tired of the

By using gunboats such as this one, the Union hoped to divide the Confederacy by taking control of the Mississippi River.

conflict and recognized the impossibility of forcing the Southern states back into the Union.

A defensive strategy made good sense for the Confederacy. First, the smaller Southern population could not field as large an army as the Union. Second, Confederate soldiers would be defending their homes, a factor that would fuel their determination to win. Third, to take the war into the Union would have meant long supply and communication lines, difficult to protect from Federal attack.

Had the South adopted a completely defensive strategy, it might well have won the war. However, proud Southerners would not support a military policy based

solely on defense, nor would they accept retreat as an integral aspect of that policy, considering such a stance cowardly. As the *Richmond Examiner* wrote, "The idea of waiting for blows, instead of inflicting them, is altogether unsuited to the genius [nature] of our people."[2]

In the end, the South adopted a defensive-offensive strategy. Whenever possible, Southern troops marched out and fought major battles with invading Northern soldiers. Further, if the opportunity presented itself, the Confederates willingly took the war to the Union by attacking the North. Because the Confederacy had practically no navy, it could do little against the Union's naval blockade.

The War Drags On

In the east, the Confederate army repeatedly beat back Union invasions, beginning on July 21, 1861, with the First Battle of Bull Run, near Manassas, Virginia. In the west, Union forces were more successful, particularly in Tennessee and along the Mississippi River. In April 1862, they captured New Orleans, the largest Confederate city.

Neither side, however, seemed able to score a victory that would end the war. Frustration at the Union's inability to smash the Confederacy mounted in the North as the war dragged on into its third year. Many in the Union were growing tired of the conflict, particularly the staggering death toll of combat. The Confederacy's strategy of wearing down the North seemed to be working.

Unlike in the North, general support for the war remained strong in the South. Southerners, like Northerners, were disturbed by the bloody cost of battle, but they saw it as a necessary price to pay to save their homes and families and preserve a way of life.

Union forces clash with the Confederates at Gettysburg. The Union victory in this battle was a turning point in the war.

The Tide Turns

At the beginning of 1863, Union morale was at an all-time low, while Southern spirits remained high. However, the tide of war changed in the summer of that year when the North scored two important victories. First, in the east, three days of fierce fighting (July 1–3) at Gettysburg, Pennsylvania, ended with the U.S. Army of the Potomac victorious over the Confederate Army of Northern Virginia and its commander, General Robert E. Lee. Second, in the west, on July 4, Union forces under the command of General Ulysses S. Grant captured the Confederate city of Vicksburg, which placed control of the entire Mississippi River in Union hands and split the Confederacy in two.

The twin defeats shocked the South, and Southern morale took a beating. Southern victory no longer seemed assured, as Confederate General Josiah Gorgas wrote:

> Events have succeeded one another with disastrous rapidity. One month ago we were apparently at the point of success. . . . Now the picture is just as somber as it was bright then. . . . Yesterday we rode on the pinnacle [summit] of success—today absolute ruin seems to be our portion.[3]

Additionally, the losses at Gettysburg and Vicksburg ended any chance that England or France would recognize the Confederacy as an independent nation or supply the South with food, arms, or equipment. The South was already suffering shortages; without outside help, these shortages became worse, particularly as the Union blockade tightened around the Confederate seacoast. The lengthening war eventually drained the desperate South's few remaining resources.

The Northern victories of 1863 showed that the Union could win the decisive battles. Only the month before the Battle of Gettysburg and the fall of Vicksburg, Northerners had all but given up on the Federal army and the war; now they were confident that the Union could and would win. In Northern cities, wrote Captain William Thompson Lusk, "Bells are ringing wildly. . . . Citizens grin at one another with fairly idiotic smiles. . . . All hysterical nonsense is pardonable now."[4] Grant was given overall command of Union forces and, after two more years of hard fighting, brought the war to an end with Lee's surrender at Appomattox Court House, Virginia, on April 9, 1865.

To Union and Confederate troops, these key events were the backdrop to their lives. They were, of course, participants in the battles, the sieges, and the occupations, but their daily concerns were more likely to be the care of their equipment, uniforms, weapons, and horses. They wanted to know what and how much there was to eat and where they would sleep. They played baseball, gambled, and sang songs to pass the time. From mundane to heroic, these were the activities that made up the days of Civil War soldiers and cavalrymen.

Chapter 1

Joining Up

The military life began for both Union and Confederate soldiers and cavalry in the same way: enlistment. Only a handful of the 3.5 million men who fought on both sides were already in the army in April 1861 when war broke out. Indeed, the standing U.S. Army comprised fewer than seventeen thousand officers and men at this time, and the recently formed Confederate army was hardly larger. The bulk of the two armies would be made up of volunteers and draftees. Some of these recruits, particularly in the South, had formerly served in the U.S. Army or state militias, but most had no military training of any kind. They signed their enlistment papers and then learned to be soldiers and cavalrymen.

How the Armies Were Organized

The large armies that the Union and Confederacy began building in 1861 were similarly organized. The basic infantry unit was the company; for the cavalry, it was the squadron or troop. Generally, ten infantry companies or five cavalry squadrons formed a regiment, and four or five regiments made up a brigade. In the South, four to five brigades composed a division; Northern divisions comprised two to three brigades. In both armies, three divisions was the normal strength of a corps.

Two or more corps made up an army group, called simply an army. One division or one corps of each army group was cavalry. In the Confederate forces, artillery units were assigned to each infantry and cavalry division. In the Federal military, part of the artillery was distributed between corps, with the remainder collected as an artillery reserve.

Union army groups tended to have more corps than did the Confederates. Thus, for example, the Union Army of the Potomac had seven corps, as opposed to the Confederate Army of Northern Virginia's three. The difference in the number of

A Northern regiment consisting of ten companies drills in camp.

corps between these groups did not mean that the Army of the Potomac was twice the size of the Army of Northern Virginia because Confederate units were larger than Union units. The average Southern infantry company or cavalry squadron had 4 officers and from 90 to 120 enlisted men. A Northern company or squadron had only 3 officers and from 80 to 95 enlisted men.

The Federals gave their army groups the names of rivers, and the Confederates, the names of regions. Thus, Union army groups included the Army of the Potomac, the Army of the Ohio, and the Army of the Cumberland. The Confederates formed the Army of Northern Virginia, the Army of Mississippi, and the Army of Tennessee, among others.

Recruiting

Neither the Union nor the Confederate armies ever did any large-scale national recruiting. Instead, each side depended on member states to supply soldiers for its ranks. These state troops were sometimes members of already established local militia, but more often, they belonged to brand-new units created in response to the war's demands. The Confederate army was composed completely of such state volunteers. The Federal army was a combination of regular army troops and state volunteers; however, the standing U.S. Army only added about ten thousand soldiers during the war, so volunteers vastly outnumbered professionals.

For the first two years of the war, the process of recruitment was much the same in the North and South. A prominent

Enlisting

Even before the war began, young Northern and Southern men began enlisting. Warren Goss describes his enlistment in the following account, taken from *The Blue and the Gray: Two Volumes in One: The Story of the Civil War as Told by Participants*, edited by Henry Steele Commager.

Before the war had . . . begun I enlisted. . . . "Cold chills" ran up and down my back as I got out of bed after . . . [a] sleepless night,

and shaved. . . . I was twenty years of age, and when anything unusual was to be done, like fighting or courting, I shaved. With a nervous tremor . . . and my heart thumping . . . , I stood before the door of the recruiting office and before turning the knob to enter, read and re-read the advertisement for recruits posted there. . . . The promised chances for "travel and promotion" seemed good. . . . I must confess that after four years of soldiering, that the "chances for travel" were no myth. But "promotion" was a little uncertain and slow.

I was in no hurry to open the door. Though determined to enlist I was half inclined to put it off awhile; I had a fluctuation [seesaw] of desires; I was fainthearted and brave; I wanted to enlist,—and yet—Here I turned the knob and was relieved. I had been more prompt, with all my hesitation, than the officer in his duty; he wasn't in.

Finally he came and said: "What do you want, my boy?"

"I want to enlist," I responded, blushing deeply with upwelling [rising] patriotism and bashfulness. . . . In justice to myself, . . . I signed the roll without a tremor.

An enlistment poster asks for "able-bodied men" to join the Union army with the promise of a $150 bounty, or reward, to each volunteer.

businessman, politician, or former army officer asked for and was given permission by his state's governor, or by either the Federal or Confederate war departments, to raise a regiment of infantry, artillery, or cavalry. This individual would then enlist assistants to sign up recruits to fill the ranks of the proposed regiment. Often whole companies would be formed by groups of friends, neighbors, or townspeople.

After 1862, instead of raising new regiments, southern states sent their recruits to existing units in need of replacements. Northern states continued creating new regiments through the entire course of the war. If an established Federal unit needed replacements, it had to send its own recruiters out to recruit them.

Taking Leave

After signing up with a regiment, a recruit had a few days to wrap up his personal affairs and say his good-byes. If he was part of a new regiment, he would join his unit, which would then travel to the state capital, national capital (Washington, D.C., for the North; Richmond, Virginia, for the South), or the nearest military training camp. Generally, if the recruit was a replacement, he was shipped with other replacements to his company in the field.

Leave-takings were emotionally mixed. One Arkansas enlistee reported that "every young fellow who went to war got a kiss from his 'best girl,' and . . . that . . . last farewell was repeated over and over again." Another recruit wrote that "scarcely could be found an eye that was not bathed in tears on this occasion."[5]

Traveling

Getting to their destinations was an adventure in itself for many recruits. One Texas company left its hometown of San Augustine in mid-September, destination Richmond. The trip began with a 120-mile hike to the Red River, where the unit boarded a ferry driven by men pushing against the river bottom with poles. From the ferry, they were transferred to a steamboat that took them to New Orleans, from which they took a train to Richmond, arriving some three weeks after they started.

Most Southern and Northern regiments did their share of train riding, which was often uncomfortable and exhausting. Civil War historian Bell Irvin Wiley writes:

> Accommodations consisted of boxcars equipped with backless benches of rough plank [wood] and, inadequately, if at all, provided with heat, ventilation, food, water and sanitary facilities. Inferior tracks and roadbeds made for rough riding. . . . On reaching their destination officers and men were sometimes so exhausted that they threw themselves on the station platform and slept for hours.[6]

Union cavalrymen, who were provided with horses after they reached their training camps or field assignments, had to walk or ride the train just like other Union soldiers.

However, according to Samuel Carter, "while the infantry traveled to Richmond by rail or trudged along dusty backroads, the [Confederate] cavalry rode from town to town with spurs and sabers jangling."[7] Southern cavalrymen, unlike Northern, were expected to report with their own horses.

Mustering In

On reaching their destination, recruits underwent a quick physical examination, which generally consisted of little more than answering a few questions from a doctor. These "exams" revealed so little that as many as a quarter of the recruits would turn out to have serious illnesses or physical disabilities that sent them to the hospital and then back home rather than to the battlefield.

After the medical exam, the men were assembled and officially mustered into service. The ceremony was basically the same for soldiers and cavalry and for North and South. The recruits took 2 oaths, the first to their home state and the second to the Federal or the Confederate government. The national oaths of allegiance were exactly the same, except for the substitution of the words "Confederate States of America" for "United States of America" in the Southern pledge. The final portion of this swearing-in ceremony was the reading of the articles of war, the military laws that would govern these men while under arms. These articles, which numbered 101, were exactly the same for both armies.

By Rail, Water, and Foot

New recruits on both sides generally had to travel long distances to reach their training camps. The following excerpt from *Soldiering: The Civil War Diary of Rice C. Bull, 123rd New York Volunteer Infantry* describes the frequently unpleasant journey of Bull and his newly formed regiment from their hometown in upstate New York to Camp Chase in Washington, D.C.

We were to go to New York city without change, so cooked rations were issued for one day, but as our haversacks [shoulder bags] were filled with good food our . . . friends had brought us from home . . . few drew these rations. . . . I am not sure where we landed in the city. . . .

After a good night's rest, we resumed our journey. . . . It was night when we reached Baltimore. . . . To reach the Washington Depot we had to march the whole length of the town. It was hot . . . and I do not think I ever suffered so much from heat and thirst. . . .

We left Baltimore but not now in passenger cars. We were packed closely in cattle cars and a hot, sweaty, hungry lot of men we were. The only food we had was what many had left over in their haversacks. . . . We were stowed away as mercilessly as if we were dumb brutes, but our patriotic ardor [enthusiasm] was running high and not many complaints were heard. . . .

When we left the train we were at once marched to the Soldiers' Home for dinner. . . . The whole Regiment was driven into and locked in an attached yard to wait until the dinner was ready. The yard was hardly large enough to hold the men and was the most filthy place I was ever in.

The recruits were now officially soldiers of their respective armies. The standard period of enlistment for most of the war was three years in both the North and South. Early on, the Union opted for a mere ninety-day enlistment period, and Confederate recruits committed to a year's service. These short obligations were based on the overly optimistic idea common to both sides that the war would be over relatively quickly. By the end of 1861, it was clear to Northerners and Southerners that the war was going to drag on for years.

Electing Officers

The next step for either a Union or Confederate volunteer company was to elect its officers, the first and second lieutenants, and its captain, the unit's commander. Then the newly elected company lieutenants and captains selected the regiment's majors and its colonel, the regiment's leader. The generals who commanded brigades and higher-level units were normally appointed by the war departments of both the Union and the Confederacy. In the North, generals were most often either active or former officers of the regular army; in the South, they were customarily officers with prior military experience.

Often, a company or regimental election was a mere formality, since the officers were already known. The regimental colonel would be the original organizer who had been given permission to raise the unit, and his assistants the other officers. However, for some companies—and even a few regiments—the election was wide open, and a period of spirited campaigning would be followed by voting.

Successful candidates often provided drinks for their unit. As one Union soldier wrote of a newly elected first lieutenant:

> [He] made a very good speech and invited us to join with him in a social glass of Brandy & water. The Col. [colonel] said that it was against the rules to allow any drinking, but as this was an especial occasion he would allow it. Our Captn and 2nd Lieut. made also some remarks, after which, and repeated cheers, we retired for the night.[8]

The losers of these elections sometimes resigned and went home.

The Draft

In the flush of patriotism following the shelling of Fort Sumter, volunteers reported by the tens of thousands. Indeed, they overwhelmed the resources of both sides, neither of which had the uniforms, weapons, or equipment to field so many enthusiastic would-be soldiers. Later, however, the situation changed drastically. As the war dragged on and casualties mounted, men on both sides became reluctant to join up. Thus, both North and South had to resort to other means to fill the ranks of their armies.

In the North, a fee known as a bounty was offered those willing to volunteer. Too often, however, paid enlistees would accept

Jumping Bounty

As the war progressed, recruits became harder to find, and the Union army began paying a fee, called a bounty, to boost enlistment. After pocketing the bounty, some recruits deserted only to reenlist, collect another bounty, and once more desert. In *Turned Inside Out: Recollections of a Private Soldier in the Army of the Potomac*, Frank Wilkeson describes his experience with bounty jumpers in 1863.

> I went to Albany and enlisted in the Eleventh New York . . . and was promptly sent out to the penitentiary building. There . . . I found eight hundred . . . ruffians, closely guarded by heavy lines of sentinels [guards] . . . , rifle in hand, to keep them [the recruits] from running away. . . . A recruit's social standing in the barracks was determined by the acts of villainy he had performed, supplemented by the number of times he had jumped the bounty. The social standing of a hard-faced, crafty pickpocket, who had jumped the bounty . . . half a dozen times, was assured. . . .
>
> On the steamboat [on route to the regiment], . . . armed sentinels stood at the openings in the vessel's sides. . . . I saw one [recruit] take off his knapsack [and] loosen his overcoat. . . . He drew a whiskey bottle from an inner pocket and repeatedly stimulated his courage. . . . At last they [the guards] turned their heads for an instant. The man sprang to his feet . . . and jumped far out into the cold waters of the river. Instantly the guards began to fire. . . . But it was exceedingly dark . . . , and I believe that the deserter escaped. . . . I was told that another recruit had jumped overboard and had been killed.

Volunteers line up in New York City to enlist and collect a bounty in the amount of $677. Some would later desert and enlist again.

the bounty and then desert as soon as possible. Some so-called bounty jumpers made a profession of enlisting, collecting the bounty, and then deserting over and over again.

Both sides were eventually forced to pass draft laws, the Confederacy in 1862 and the North in 1863. Numerous loopholes, however, allowed many to escape the draft. In both North and South, a draftee could pay a tax, $500 in the South, $300 in the North, to be excused from the draft. Another allowable practice was paying a substitute to enter the army in a draftee's place. Consequently, many wealthy men were able to avoid military service, leading to the charge that it was "a rich man's war and a poor man's fight."[9]

Discriminatory draft practices created much bitterness in the Union and the Confederacy alike. In New York City, on Sunday, July 12, 1863, a week after the Battle of Gettysburg, this resentment flared into the worst riot in U.S. history. The rioters, mobs of poor protesting the draft, rampaged for four days, looting and burning Federal buildings, particularly draft offices. U.S. troops finally put down the riot, which left over a hundred dead.

A blindfolded man pulls draft numbers at a conscription station in New York. At first relying on volunteers, both sides eventually had to pass draft laws.

Young and Old Go to War

In general, Civil War soldiers were young men between the ages of eighteen and twenty-nine. However, many middle-aged and even older men carried arms. The Union's 37th Iowa Regiment included almost 150 men over sixty. Known as the Graybeards, this unit performed guard duty. Its oldest member, and the oldest soldier on either side, was eighty-year-old Curtis King, who served for a few months before being discharged for disability in 1863.

Young boys also managed to enlist despite the stated minimum age in both armies of eighteen. Most underage soldiers were teenagers, thirteen to seventeen, but the Confederate Charles C. Hay was eleven, and the Federalist Edward Black, an astonishing nine. Many of these youngsters were drummer boys, although some, such as the fifteen-year-old Southerner John Roberts, actually fought in battle. To avoid outright lying, many of these boys would write "18" on a piece of paper, slip it into a shoe, and swear that they were over eighteen.

Who the Soldiers Were

Union and Confederate soldiers and cavalrymen came from all walks of life. As scholar James I. Robertson writes, "From farms and factories, schools and shops—from every byway and highway in the land, they came by tens of thousands to answer the call to arms."[10]

Filling the ranks of Northern and Southern infantry and artillery companies were farmers, blacksmiths, peddlers, sailors, bartenders, musicians, miners, and even professional gamblers, to name just a few. The urban Northerners tended to be more varied than the rural Southerners. Union rosters often listed as many as three hundred occupations, compared with an average of one hundred for Confederate units. Wiley notes that

> The occupational diversity which characterized the Union forces gave them a resourcefulness which stood them in good stead in camp, on the march, and during battle. If a wagon, steamboat, or locomotive broke down, more than likely some soldier could be found close at hand who knew how to make it go again. . . . When a Southern town was captured and the occupying [Northern] forces wanted a newspaper, they called out printers from their own ranks . . . , as did the First Minnesota at Berryville, Virginia.[11]

Southerners Take to War

Union cavalry regiments tended to reflect the same variety of occupations as did the infantry and artillery. However, what most Federal cavalry recruits lacked was riding experience. Stephen Z. Starr observes that

If there was a common denominator for the men and boys of the Union cavalry, it was their lack of ability to ride or take care of a horse. In the North, unlike the South, horses were driven, not ridden. The extent of the riding skill even of most boys raised on Northern farms was to sit bareback on the broad rump of a plow horse as it ambled back to the barn after a day's work in the fields.[12]

Confederate cavalry units, on the other hand, were drawn mostly from the Southern aristocracy, virtually all of whom had been riding since childhood. Union general William Sherman described Southern horse soldiers as "the young bloods of the South, sons of planters . . . and sportsmen. . . . They are splendid riders, first-rate shots, and utterly reckless."[13] Thus, at the beginning of the war, Confederates were far better horsemen than Federals.

Steeped in a strong military tradition, Southerners were in general more skilled than Northerners in military matters. For example, Southerners made up the majority of every prewar class at the U.S. Military Academy at West Point, and the South supported a number of its own military academies, such as the Virginia Military Institute, where Confederate general Stonewall Jackson was teaching at the beginning of the war. Additionally, there were more Southern state militias than Northern, and these Southern units tended to be better-trained and -equipped than their Northern counterparts. These advantages, however, would not last as the war continued and Union soldiers and cavalry learned the lessons of warfare.

They Also Fought

Both armies also included many immigrants and foreign nationals, understandably in greater numbers in the Union army since almost a third of the male population of that region was foreign born, compared with only 9 percent of the population of the South. Several thousand Englishmen and Canadians were enlisted by both the North and South, and both sides fielded German and Irish regiments. Union units also included the Scandinavian 15th Wisconsin and the French 55th New York, called the La Garde Lafayette (the Lafayette Guard).

Both sides also had mixed European regiments. Serving in the North was the 39th New York, known as the Garibaldi Guards. Led by the Hungarian-born Frederick George D'Utassy, this regiment had companies of Germans, Hungarians, Swiss,

Most Southerners grew up riding horses and shooting rifles, giving them an advantage over Northerners at the start of the war.

War Meeting

Recruiters in both the North and the South enticed men to join the army through war meetings. In *Hardtack and Coffee: The Unwritten Story of Army Life*, former Army of the Potomac private John D. Billings describes the general course of such an event.

> War meetings . . . were designed to stir lagging enthusiasm. Musicians and orators [speakers] blew themselves red in the face with their windy efforts. Choirs improvised [organized] for the occasion sang . . . til too hoarse for further endeavor. The old veteran soldier of [the War of] 1812 was trotted out, and worked for all he was worth. . . . At proper intervals the enlistment roll would be presented for signatures. There was generally one old fellow present who . . . would yell like a hyena, and declare his readiness to shoulder his musket and go, if he wasn't so old. . . . Then there was a patriotic maiden lady [unmarried older woman] who kept a flag or a handkerchief waving . . . , who 'would go in a minute if she was a man.' Besides these there was usually a man who would [pledge to be] one of fifty [volunteers] . . . to enlist when he well understood that such a number could not be obtained. And there was one more often found present who when challenged to sign would agree to, *provided* that A or B (men of wealth) would put down *their* names. . . .
>
> Sometimes the patriotism of such a gathering would be wrought up so intensely . . . that a town's quota would be filled in less than an hour. It needed only the first man to . . . put down his name . . . and be cheered . . . as the hero of the hour, when a second, a third, a fourth would follow, and at last a perfect stampede.

Sheet music to a patriotic song is dedicated to "All Who Love Our Country." Such music would be sung at war meetings to encourage recruitment.

Italians, French, Spanish, and Portuguese. The unit's officers had to give orders in a variety of languages. The South fielded a similar regiment, commanded by the French count Camille Armand Jules Marie, Prince de Polignac, later affectionately dubbed the Polecat by the Texans he led.

Native Americans also served in the Civil War. The Confederacy formed three brigades of Cherokee, Choctaw, Chickasaw, and Seminole, while the Union possessed one brigade of Creek. Their activities were

mostly confined to the region west of the Mississippi River, close to the Oklahoma Indian Territories.

Black Americans Fight for the Union

At the beginning of the war, many African Americans were anxious to enlist and fight for the Union. Although slavery did not exist in the North, except in the border states of Delaware, Maryland, Kentucky, and Missouri, racial prejudice did. So, although blacks often were employed as laborers, they could not enlist in the Federal army, many of whose soldiers were hostile to the idea of black troops.

At first, blacks could not serve in the Union military. After the Emancipation Proclamation, they were allowed to join the army (pictured) or navy.

After Lincoln issued the Emancipation Proclamation on September 22, 1862, abolitionists were finally able to win the right for African Americans to serve in the Union army. The first black combat units were formed the next year, although their officers remained white, and black troops were paid less than white troopers.

One of the most famous of these regiments was the 54th Massachusetts Infantry, headed by Colonel Robert Gould Shaw, a member of one of the most active anti-slavery families in New England. Among others serving in the 54th Massachusetts were two sons of Frederick Douglass, the former slave who became one of America's most effective speakers and writers against slavery.

Despite the good combat record of two African American regiments in Louisiana in the spring of 1863, Shaw had difficulty winning the right for his men to fight. Finally, on July 18, 1863, the 54th Massachusetts joined the attack on Fort Wagner, near Charleston, South Carolina. Although the 54th, at the head of the attacking Federals,

A memorial in Boston depicts Colonel Robert Gould Shaw (on horseback) and his all-black 54th Massachusetts Infantry.

took heavy casualties, it proved that African American soldiers were as brave and capable as any of their white comrades.

Among those killed was Colonel Shaw, whom the Confederates buried in a mass grave with his men. Offended that the Union accepted blacks in combat, they meant the gesture as an insult. Shaw's parents, however, were pleased, saying that their son would have wanted to be buried with the men whom he had led and with whom he had died.

The example of the 54th Massachusetts spurred the creation of other African American regiments. Before the war ended, more than a hundred black units of infantry, cavalry, and artillery saw action. But before any Northern or Southern soldier or cavalryman saw action, he first had to be outfitted and trained.

Chapter 2

Uniforms and Rifles

In both the Union and the Confederacy, adequate outfitting of recruits and seasoned troops—that is, issuing uniforms, weapons, and equipment and replacing lost, worn-out, or destroyed items—was essential. In general, the industrialized North had an easier job of outfitting than did the rural South, where coping with shortages of everything became a way of life.

On both sides, it was common practice for officers and men to add to or to replace standard issue uniforms, weapons, and other equipment at their own expense. Nonetheless, as do most armies, both Federal and Confederate armies specified regulation dress and gear, with which all soldiers became familiar.

Federal Uniforms

Union and Confederate armies both issued a dress code, although not all soldiers and cavalry followed it. Federal infantry officers and men were issued a long dress coat of dark blue wool and a dark blue jacket, known as a blouse, which

Federal officers' uniforms included dress coats, kepis, and broad-brimmed hats.

most preferred to the dress coat. Additionally, they were given light blue pants, a dark wool shirt, socks, and drawers, long underpants that protected the legs from chafing by the trousers when marching. Each infantryman also received rugged black shoes, called gunboats by the soldiers. The most common hat was a kepi, a cap with a visor and a round, flat top that slopes forward. These were also called forage caps. Broad-brimmed hats were also worn.

Union cavalry dress was much the same as for the infantry. However, the horse soldiers were issued shorter jackets, boots instead of shoes, and pants that were reinforced in the seat and legs for riding. Artillery personnel wore the same uniform as the cavalry, since they rode horses alongside their guns on the march.

Federal Insignia

Officers fastened rank insignia to shoulder straps, while noncommissioned officers—that is, sergeants and corporals—sewed chevrons to the sleeve. The buttons of enlisted men's uniforms were stamped with a spread eagle, while those of officers were marked *I*, *C*, or *A* for infantry, cavalry, and artillery, respectively.

The uniform cap of officers and noncommissioned officers was embroidered with either a blue bugle for infantry, yellow crossed sabers for cavalry, or red crossed cannons for artillery. Additionally, affixed to the front of the cap was a brass number indicating the wearer's regiment seated above a letter indicating his company. On

their caps, Federal privates had brass bugles, sabers, or cannons, depending on their branch, along with brass numbers and letters.

Confederate Dress

A Confederate infantry soldier was issued pants, a white cotton shirt, drawers, socks, shoes, and a kepi. The Southern uniform

This Confederate soldier is wearing the standard uniform of short gray jacket and striped pants.

code originally called for a long gray coat, but it was soon replaced by a short gray jacket that reached only to the waist and which gave the name Gray Jackets to these troops. Regulations called for light blue trousers, with a red stripe running down each leg of officers' uniforms. In practice, officers and men alike ignored this regulation and wore gray pants. Cavalry and artillery regulation uniforms were much the same as those for the infantry, with modifications like those of the Union army.

The Confederates used the same color code as the Federals to indicate service branch, with a kepi's crown being so colored as to show the wearer's service. Buttons with *I*, *C*, or *A* standing for infantry, cavalry, and artillery, also identified the service branch of officers and men. Officers fastened their rank insignia to the collar and to the sleeve, while noncommissioned officers, like their Northern counterparts, wore chevrons on the sleeve.

Dressing to Please

Union troops tended to follow the uniform code more closely than did Confederates. As one British observer noted after reviewing an Arkansas unit:

The men were . . . well clothed, though without any attempt at uniformity in color or cut; but nearly all were dressed in gray or brown coats and . . . hats.

I was told that even if a regiment was clothed in proper uniform by the gov-

ernment, it would become parti-colored [many colored] again in a week, as the soldiers preferred wearing the . . . home-spun jackets and trousers made by their mothers and sisters. . . . The generals very wisely allow them to please themselves in this respect.[14]

Even the generals followed this informal uniform practice. Robert E. Lee almost always wore a civilian frock coat.

Confederate cavalry units were particularly fond of nonregulation uniforms. They saw themselves as swashbuckling heroes, and Carter writes that, in keeping with this dashing image, "they created their own uniforms in every shade of blue and gray, with a penchant [liking] for gold and scarlet trimmings—braided jackets, silk-lined capes, soft broad-brimmed hats, and hussar [thigh-high] boots."[15] The well-known cavalry commander General James E. B. "Jeb" Stuart favored a scarlet-lined jacket; yellow sash, tied with gold tassels; elbow-length gloves; ostrich-plumed hat; and gold spurs.

Union cavalry tended to be much less colorful than Confederate, although members of the 3rd New Jersey added extra braid to their jackets and wore hussar boots and a yellow-lined cape, for which finery they were called the Butterflies. Union cavalry general George Armstrong Custer rode to battle in a black velvet, gold-trimmed jacket and pants; a blue shirt with wide collar, upon which were silver stars; and a crimson scarf tied around his neck.

More Fancy Dress

At the beginning of the war, neither side was consistent in its uniforms, and a variety of styles appeared during the first year of fighting. Militia units often wore their pre-war dress, and many volunteer regiments wore uniforms of their own design, assembled for them by wives, mothers, and sisters.

Among Confederate troops, Irish volunteers from Mobile, Alabama, wore green; an infantry company from North Carolina favored red shirts and black pants; and a company from Tennessee was decked out in yellow, earning it the name Yellow Jackets. Among the Union boys, a New York regiment known as the Highlanders wore plaid and the Garibaldi Guards adopted red shirts, dark-blue pants and coats, and a rounded, full-brimmed hat with a plume of black feathers.

The most colorful of all nonregulation uniforms, however, was that worn by Zouave infantry regiments. The Zouave uniform was modeled on the dress of French infantry serving in Algiers, the name Zouave taken from a people native to the mountains of that country. This uniform generally had a short blue jacket, trimmed with gold lace, ribbons, and buttons; a blue shirt, open and low cut; scarlet pantaloons, that is, baggy pants tied at the ankles; yellow leggings; and a blue sash.

These Union soldiers are sporting Zouave uniforms, with baggy pantaloons, gold-trimmed jackets, and kepis.

Headgear—either a turban, a fez, a tasseled cap, or a kepi—was always red.

Both Federals and Confederates adopted Zouave uniforms, causing confusion on the battlefield. At the First Battle of Bull Run, Confederate general Jeb Stuart mistook a New York Zouave regiment for a friendly one from Louisiana; before he discovered his mistake, he and his command were fired on by the Federals.

Similar confusion resulted from other uniform choices, as well. Also at the First Battle of Bull Run, some Southern troops were wearing blue and some Union forces gray, drawing friendly fire.

A major disadvantage of Zouave and other colorful uniforms was that they stood out in battle, and thus their wearers became easy targets, leading to high casualties among many nonregulation units. For these reasons, the fancy uniforms were mostly discarded by the end of the first year of the conflict, although some Northern companies retained the Zouave costume until the end of the war.

The Springfield Rifle

After uniforms were issued—and sometimes before—came weapons, of which the most important in the war was the infantry rifle. Both Confederate and Federal infantry units used many different types of rifles during the Civil War, but the most common was the Springfield, named for Springfield, Massachusetts, where most of the guns were manufactured. The Union army made or bought some 1.5 million

Springfields during the Civil War. The South depended on stocks of rifles taken from Federal arsenals that were now in Confederate territory or captured during battles and raids, but did produce some Springfields at the Confederate Armory in Richmond, Virginia.

The Springfield was technically a riflemusket because its barrel was longer and thinner than a true rifle's. It weighed nine pounds and measured five feet in length, over six feet with bayonet fixed. It fired a single shot and was accurate up to a quarter mile. At close range—anything under a thousand feet—it was deadly, as this description by Confederate general John Gordon confirms: "My [unit's] rifles flamed and roared in the Federal's faces. . . . The effect was appalling [horrible]. The entire front line . . . went down in the . . . blast."[16]

To load the Springfield, a soldier took from a belt pouch a cartridge, a paper-wrapped package holding gunpowder and a bullet. He bit off the powder end and poured the powder down the barrel, then pushed in the bullet after the powder with a ramrod. Experienced soldiers could load and fire three times a minute.

A nervous or exhausted soldier sometimes loaded his rifle incorrectly and put the gun out of action. He might put the bullet in and then the powder. He might jam several cartridges down the barrel. (One rifle found on the Gettysburg battlefield had been loaded with twenty-three cartridges!) Or he might simply forget to take out the ramrod and shoot it away.

Supplying Arms

In the following account, reprinted in *The Blue and the Gray*, edited by Henry Steele Commager, Edward P. Alexander, chief of ordnance for the Army of Northern Virginia, describes how he supplied Robert E. Lee's army with guns and ammunition and how the army eventually updated its infantry weapons.

Briefly, my duties embraced the supply of arms and ammunition to all troops in the field—infantry, artillery, and cavalry. I organized the department, with an . . . officer or sergeant in every regiment, from whom I received weekly statements showing the arms and ammunition on hand in cartridge boxes and regimental wagons. Reserve storehouses [of arms] were provided at the nearest railroad points, and . . . trains . . . to run between the storehouses and the troops. For emergency, . . . was held a train of ammunition . . . and wagons equipped with tools and expert mechanics for all sorts of repairs. . . .

In the early stages we had great trouble with the endless variety of arms and calibres [ammunition size] in use, scarcely ten per cent of them being the muzzle-loading rifle musket [Springfield], calibre .58. . . .

The old smooth-bore [lacking rifling] musket, calibre .69, made up the bulk of the Confederate armament at the beginning, some of the guns . . . being old flint-locks. But every effort was made to replace them by rifled muskets captured in battle, brought through the blockade . . . , or manufactured at a few small arsenals which we gradually fitted up. Not until after the Battle of Gettysburg [1863] was the whole army of Virginia equipped with the rifled musket.

The markings on these vintage Civil War ammunition boxes show that they contain bullets and cartridges for Springfield rifles.

After a battle, a soldier was expected to clean his rifle. He filled the barrel with warm water, plugged up the ends, and shook it to agitate the water. Next, a rag attached to the ramrod was run through the barrel. The soldier finished the job by scouring the exterior of the barrel and other metal fittings with an abrasive such as ashes or emery.

Cavalry Carbines

The cavalry used a much lighter weight, shorter barreled rifle, called a carbine. With their shortened barrels, carbines had an effective range of only 450 to 600 feet, sufficient, however, for the type of close-in fighting required of horse soldiers.

Several types of carbines found use in the Civil War, but Union cavalry favored the Sharps and the Spencer. Unlike the Springfield, these guns were breechloaders; that is, ammunition was fed into the barrel from the rear through the rifle's breech. In the Sharps, a soldier pushed the trigger forward, thereby moving a block and exposing the bore, or the rifled tunnel in the barrel through which the bullet traveled. A linen-jacketed cartridge was slipped into place and the breech closed. The Sharps fired three times more rapidly then the Springfield.

The Spencer was a repeater and could fire eight shots before having to be reloaded. The rate of fire was about five times that of the Springfield. Its metal-jacketed cartridges nestled in a tube in the rifle's shoulder stock and were fed into the firing chamber by a lever. The

Favored by the cavalry, the Spencer repeating rifle could fire eight shots without needing to be reloaded.

Spencer, which was some three feet in length, was a prized cavalry weapon, and was also used by some infantry troops.

Confederate cavalry appreciated the advantage of the Spencer, but could only use the repeaters as long as they had Federal ammunition because Southern armories lacked the technology to manufacture the specialized Spencer cartridge. Most Confederate horse soldiers made do with a shortened muzzle-loading Springfield or other infantry rifle. They also used stolen Sharps or a Confederate imitation. Southern armories were able to supply the ammunition for this breechloader.

Revolvers and Swords

Various types of handguns were toted in the Civil War, but the favorite was the six-shot Colt revolver. Colt manufactured two versions: a navy issue and an army model that took a larger cartridge. Both models were carried by Union and Confederate army officers (Confederates using either stolen Federal arms or Southern copies). All members of the cavalry, North and South, wore pistols, although when issued

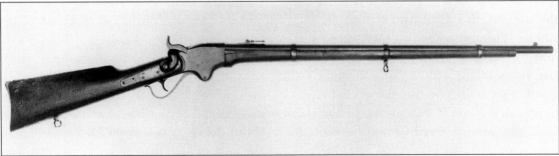

A highly decorated Colt revolver lies in a case with its accessories. Standard issue Colts were not so ornate.

Fully Equipped

Along with guns, swords, and bayonets, soldiers and cavalry of both sides were issued a range of other gear. Large items included knapsacks and blankets, one wool, one rubber to keep off the rain. Each soldier received a leather cartridge box fastened to a shoulder strap; the divided tin interior of the box could hold sixty rounds. Canteens were issued, canvas-covered metal for Federals, wood for Confederates. Troops were also given a second shoulder bag, called a haversack, in which they carried food. Eating utensils, a plate, and a cup were hooked to the belt.

A fully equipped and fully armed infantryman or cavalryman carried forty to fifty pounds of regulation gear, including his weapons. Much of this weight and equipment was shed as troops gained experience, reducing the load to some thirty pounds, for as Confederate general Richard Ewell said, "The road to glory cannot be followed with much baggage."[18]

Thus, a rolled blanket slung from shoulder to waist, instead of a knapsack and haversack, easily carried personal effects and food. Cartridges were stuffed into pockets. Some men even threw away their canteens, using their cups to drink

breech-loading carbines, the horse soldiers found them the more effective battlefield weapon.

Federal and Confederate officers, as well as some sergeants and corporals, carried swords. Cavalry units were also issued a heavy, curved type of sword known as a saber. Swords, indeed all cutting weapons such as bayonets and knives, proved of little use on the Civil War battleground, where rifle and artillery power were the keys to victory. Even in hand-to-hand combat, notes Wiley, soldiers "much preferred grabbing the gun by the barrel and clubbing with the butt."[17] Not even 1 percent of Civil War wounds were caused by swords, knives, or bayonets.

out of streams and springs. Discarded also were extra clothing and coats since most of the fighting took place in warm weather. Even the cavalry stripped down to make their load lighter on their horses for faster movement. In the end, as one Confederate observed,

> Reduced to the minimum, the private soldier consisted of one man, one hat, one jacket, one shirt, one pair of pants, one pair of drawers, one pair of shoes, and one pair of socks. His baggage was one blanket.[19]

Cavalry Needs

In addition to uniforms, weapons, and standard equipment, cavalry units needed both horses and horse tack, such as saddles and harnesses. At the beginning of the war, both Federal and Confederate war departments required that each cavalry trooper provide his own mount and tack. According to Starr, the "[U.S.] government paid the owner forty cents a day for the use of the horse, supplied the feed, and paid the appraised [determined] value of the animal if it was killed in battle—but not if it died of disease, starvation, or overwork."[20] The Confederate government's policy was the same.

Though a number of Northern regiments were raised under these terms, in general the policy failed in the North because many recruits lacked both a horse and the means to buy one. By August 1861 the Union war department began supply-

Equipment Inventory

Both Union and Confederate soldiers started out loaded with equipment, issued and personal, but with experience they threw much of it away. In James I. Robertson's *Soldiers Blue and Gray*, George Allen, a member of the 4th Rhode Island, inventories his gear as a recruit and then as a veteran campaigner.

There was a full supply of underclothing, woolen blanket, rubber [blanket], three or four pairs of socks, half a dozen nice handkerchiefs, dress coat, fatigue cap [forage cap], supply of ink, letter paper and envelopes, . . . photograph album, Bible, the journal in which these notes are kept, tobacco, . . . comb and brush, shaving tools, two or three pipes, pins and needles, thread, buttons, etc., and other things. . . . Add to these, . . . haversack with rations, mostly obtained from home, . . . consisting of cold meats, bread and butter, cheese, pie and cake. . . . Then there was the canteen . . . ; and then there were patent water filters, knife and fork, spoon, cup and plate, shoe brush and blacking [polish], various kinds of medicine, and flannels for sudden changes of climate or weather, a pair of warm mittens for coming winter. . . . Everything . . . thought necessary to our new life as a soldier. . . .

What a difference one year in service made. . . . A woolen blanket and a piece of shelter tent twisted together and thrown over our shoulder; . . . little bag of coffee and sugar . . . ; little to eat, but plenty of ammunition; dirty and ragged. . . . But we were soldiers then.

ing both mounts and riding equipment to cavalry units. The suitability of these horses, however, was dubious. One member of the 1st New York wrote that [these mounts] were of the very worst description, and not one of six of them fit for the cavalry service. They were of bad stock, many of them blemished beyond cure, and of an age that showed that they should have long since been sent to die in a different and less hazardous service. . . . Many of these horses had evidently been nursed into tolerably good condition externally, but they would show their defects and break down under the least hardship or exposure.[21]

By no means were all lots of horses this bad, and in general, the Union system of supplying horses, as well as replacement mounts, worked to keep Northern troopers riding.

The Confederates retained the old policy of trooper-provided mounts, and it hurt them during the last years of the war. The South had a smaller overall supply of horses than did the North, and as horse casualties climbed, a severe horse shortage plagued the region. Even when a cavalryman could find a horse, demand often priced it beyond his ability to buy. A cavalry trooper on foot soon found himself transferred to the infantry.

Shortages

Horses were not the only items in short supply during the Civil War. And although shortages affected the Southern army far more than the Northern, both Union and Confederate troops suffered from them.

Warfare is hard on both clothes and shoes. Shoes were among the most important possessions of both Union and Confederate infantrymen, but long marches to and from battle, particularly in rough country, quickly wore out even sturdy issue footwear. Confederate soldiers had increasing difficulty in getting new shoes as the conflict wore on and Southern resources dwindled. Many found themselves barefoot even in winter. Some made footwear out of green cowhide, which did not hold its shape well and began to rot soon after it was fashioned. Others found replacements by taking the shoes from dead Federals or Union prisoners.

Indeed, many Confederates found it necessary to use bits and pieces of Federal uniforms to replace the rags of their own worn-out clothing. Such seizure usually meant that the cloth had to be bleached white to remove the blue. Union blankets were also a prize sought by Confederates, many of whom were forced to use pieces of carpet to replace their own lost or threadbare blankets. It was a rare Confederate cavalry raid whose sole objective was to strike a blow against Union troops. In general, Southern horse soldiers were always looking to steal Federal supplies.

Replacing worn-out shoes and uniforms was sometimes difficult even for the better-supplied Federal army. Both the Antietam and Gettysburg campaigns left many Union soldiers shoeless. After

Needed Repairs

Southern resources were limited, and the Confederate army was unable to replace worn-out, damaged, or lost supplies. In *The Blue and the Gray*, edited by Henry Steele Commager, McHenry Howard, an officer of the Army of Northern Virginia, explains how soldiers spent their winters in repairs.

A number of shoemakers in the different regiments . . . were encouraged to send home . . . for their tools, and were put to work repairing shoes, being exempted from guard and other routine camp duty, but ready to fall into their commands [units] on any call to arms. The shoe-shops were a separate camp of tents. . . . A careful estimate and report of the saving of the issue of shoes . . . was made to the higher authorities. . . . The saving was . . . several hundred pairs; besides, the men's feet were kept in better condition by the correction of ill-fitting shoes. . . .

[Mechanics] were detailed to put the ambulances . . . and transportation [wagons] generally in good order. . . . General Steuart [sic] had also detailed . . . tinners [metal workers] to mend . . . cups and other tinware. . . .

The General [Robert E. Lee] was . . . desirous of establishing 'tailor shops' to patch and mend clothes . . . and sent up urgent applications for waste odds and ends of cloth and thread at the government factories, but had received no response when the opening of the Spring campaign put a check to these and many other schemes.

In short, recognizing the straits that the Confederacy was now put to in the furnishing of supplies, we aimed to save and eke out issues [conserve issued goods] in every possible way.

Unable to replace damaged equipment, the Confederate army relied on the services of blacksmiths (pictured) to make repairs.

Antietam, one Northern soldier wrote that "I saw men with no coats, no underclothes, in rags, no shoes."[22]

The Causes of Shortages

For the Federals, shortages were most common at the beginning of the war, when war industries had not yet geared up to meet army needs. Another source of shortages was war profiteering. Cheap and inferior materials were sometimes used in the production of Federal uniforms and shoes by dishonest manufacturers seeking a fast buck. Such shoddy goods fell apart quickly and supplies would thus be drained more rapidly than expected, leading to shortfalls.

In the South, shortages arose in part because Confederate industry was too meager to meet army demands, and partly as a result of the Union blockade that kept goods from reaching the South.

Moreover, even when raw materials were available, labor was not. Thus, during the winter of 1862, two thousand Confederate soldiers were assigned to do nothing but make shoes. Women all over the Confederacy, including the wife and daughters of Robert E. Lee, made socks for Southern troops. Some women even managed to turn out whole uniforms.

One result of these Southern shortages was a change in the color of Confederate uniforms from gray to yellowish brown known as butternut. After 1863 the blockade reduced supplies of the cadet-gray dye needed to color Southern uniforms. Confederate cloth producers turned to a homemade dye made from walnut shells and copperas, a substance produced by soaking rusty iron in water. Butternut-colored uniforms became more common than gray, particularly among enlisted personnel, as the war dragged on.

Uniforms and weapons were the trappings of the Northern and Southern soldiers' world, and indeed, could not make

This magazine cover from 1861 illustrates war production at a Federal arsenal. The war industry in the North was not yet ready to meet army needs.

soldiers of untrained men. As in all wars, during the Civil War, training and discipline were essential in turning hundreds of thousands of former civilians into soldiers and cavalrymen.

Chapter 3

Training and Discipline

Neither the Union nor the Confederacy had a formal, standardized training program for recruits. Historian William J. Miller writes that "in the Civil War, there were no such things as [sending] a soldier . . . to a permanent military base to go

Federal troops drill in a training camp in New York at the start of the war. Like many other camps, this one is made up of hastily constructed buildings and tents.

through a prescribed [assigned] number of weeks of basic training before being shipped out. The soldier of the Civil War received a more haphazard training."[23]

Camps of Rendezvous and Instruction

Most Northern and Southern states did set up camps to which infantry, artillery, and cavalry recruits were routed before being

sent off to join their brigades. These camps of rendezvous, as they were called, popped up in vacant lots, fairgrounds, town and city parks, and even open prairies. They were places to assemble volunteers and organize them into companies and regiments rather than train the individual to become a soldier and few of them lasted more than a few months.

A few states set up more permanent camps of instruction, which served as training centers. One of the most well known camps of instruction was Camp Curtin, outside Harrisburg, Pennsylvania. The length of time any recruit stayed in these training camps varied from a few hours to months and depended solely on the need for replacements in the field.

Disease and Death

None of these camps was elegant; makeshift buildings, if there were buildings, let in rain and winter winds. Many early recruits found themselves assembled on bare fields with hammers, saws, and nails, ordered to build barracks for themselves.

The camps also were breeding grounds for disease. The cursory medical exams given recruits failed to weed out sufferers of contagious diseases such as smallpox, measles, and whooping cough. Many recruits were farm boys who had spent much of their life isolated from large groups of people and, thus, had not developed immunity to common childhood diseases that often proved fatal to the adult soldier. Poor sanitation was another source of sickness, as-

sociated with typhoid fever, among other diseases.

Disease, in fact, was the greatest killer of Northern and Southern troops: Two-thirds of Union deaths and three-fourths of Confederate deaths were the result of unchecked illness.

Quality of Training

In general, troops on both sides received some training before seeing combat. Only a few units of green hands actually made it to the front lines without any instruction whatever.

However, the extent of training that newly formed companies or regiments received varied drastically. Outfits commanded by men with sound military experience, whether gained in the U.S. Army or state militia, often received good training from day one.

In too many units, however, officers as unskilled as their men had to scramble to learn before they could instruct. One inexperienced Confederate lieutenant wrote, "Oh! that I could have . . . gone to school for two or three months as a . . . student of the company . . . drills, learning to give and superintend [supervise] the execution of the commands belonging to my new office!"[24]

Michigan's Fort Wayne was one of the rare camps of instruction that provided the schooling for which the above lieutenant yearned. A unit's officers and noncoms would arrive ahead of its privates and take turns drilling each other. By the time the

General George McClellan believed that the key to a successful army was rigorous training and discipline.

hands of army-assigned veterans. Again, training quality varied. One of the best-trained groups during the war was the Army of the Potomac, whose first commanding officer, General George McClellan, believed that military success depended on highly trained and disciplined troops.

It was also McClellan who unsuccessfully urged the Union war department to disperse regular army personnel among all volunteer units to instruct and guide them. The war department preferred instead to keep the regular army units intact, reasoning that the professionals would be less likely to panic or desert under fire than the volunteers and thus would be a steadying, or calming, influence on the battlefield. A few old army hands were assigned from time to time as instructors, but in general, this role was filled by seasoned volunteers.

rest of the outfit arrived, the leaders were familiar with military procedure.

Training sometimes improved when the soldiers and cavalry were sent to join their brigades. There they came under direct Federal or Confederate control, in the

The School of the Soldier

To train infantry recruits, both Union and Confederate armies depended initially on Winfield Scott's 1835 *Infantry Tactics* and a later book, William J. Hardee's *Rifle and Infantry Tactics*. In 1862 the Federal army adopted Silas Casey's three-volume *Infantry Tactics, for the Instruction, Exercise, and Manouevers of the Soldier.*

The Awkward Squad

Many recruits, North and South, found army training a trial, but none so much as the awkward squad, described here in *Hardtack and Coffee*, the reminiscences of John D. Billings.

There were scores of men who spoke English who would "hay-foot" [move the left foot] every time when they should "straw-foot" [move the right foot]. They were incorrigibles [hopeless] in almost every military respect. Whenever they were out . . . for drill, they made business lively enough for the sergeant in charge. When they stood in the rear rank their loftiest ambition seemed to be to walk up the backs of their file-leaders, and then they would insist that it was the file-leaders who were out of step. . . .

To see such men attempt to change step while marching was no mean show. . . . And if such a squad under full headway were surprised with a sudden command to halt, they went all to pieces. It was no easy task to align [straighten] them. . . .

The awkward squad excelled equally in the . . . manual-of-arms [handling their rifle-muskets]. . . . At a "shoulder" [command to rest the rifle on the shoulder] their muskets pointed at all angles, from forty-five degrees to a vertical. In the attempt to change to a "carry," a part of them would drop their muskets. . . . But, with all their awkwardness and slowness at becoming acquainted with a soldier's duties, the recruits . . . behaved manfully. They made a poor exhibition on the parade ground, but could generally be counted on when more serious work was at hand.

Each of these manuals began with a section called "The School of the Soldier," which taught such basics as how to stand erect, how to face right or left, and how to salute. Additionally, recruits learned the various orders of marching: forward, to the rear, diagonally, and by the flank. Finally, they were instructed in carrying, loading, and firing their rifles, as well as thrusting with the bayonet.

Marching

Even the most elementary maneuvers proved difficult for recruits. Marching in step posed a problem because, it turned out, many did not know their right foot from their left. Drill instructors solved this problem by having the recruits attach a piece of hay to the left shoe and a piece of straw to the right. The instructor would then call out "hayfoot, strawfoot," instead of "left, right."

Even facing left—that is, turning left— or facing right were troublesome. As one Union soldier remembered:

The drill in the "facings" disclosed the fact that many, otherwise intelligent men were not certain as to which was their right hand or their left. Consequently, when the order "Right Face!" was given, [instead of facing the back of the next recruit's head] face met face in inquiring astonishment, and frantic attempts to obey the order properly made still greater confusion.[25]

Load and Fire

Learning to handle their rifles was one of the new soldiers' most physically demanding tasks. Just lifting the heavy Springfields into the straight-out firing position took muscle power, and drillmasters routinely made the men hold this position while they adjusted muzzles up and down until the rifles were even.

Loading was a particularly complicated procedure, described by Scott in twelve steps, by Hardee and Casey in nine. At least one Union officer, while instructing his unit in loading, admitted that he could not do it himself. Most recruits learned to load by first going through the motions without live ammunition.

Target practice was a rarity on both sides. A very few Federal and Confederate companies and regiments had formal target practice; more commonly, small groups of men would occasionally sneak off and shoot at barrels and tree branches. However, even these informal sessions were difficult to arrange since commanding officers often refused to issue ammunition; too many inexperienced soldiers accidentally shot each other, at a cost of eyes, fingers, and even lives.

In large part because of this lack of target practice, Civil War soldiers, North and South, were poor marksmen.

Both formal and informal testing revealed that Southern and Northern soldiers only hit the target one in three times. One Confederate observed that if his unit mates shot as well at the enemy as at a barrel target, they would not hit many Federals.

The Training Continues

The school of the soldier was followed by the school of the company, in which the soldiers learned to maneuver as a company. The recruits were taught to move back and forth from the standard marching formation, a column four abreast, to the battlefield formation, two advancing lines of soldiers, one behind the other.

This infantry company is learning the battlefield formation, in which soldiers advance in two lines, one behind the other.

The school of the regiment, in which companies learned to function as a unit, generally completed a recruit's instruction. In theory, there were also schools of the brigade and the division, but such training was rare.

Simulated combat drills were also unusual during Civil War training. Occasionally, a brigade commander would divide his infantry, cavalry, and artillery into two sides, issue blank ammunition, and play war. As one Union soldier said, "The Cavalry charged down on us, and for the first time I saw something that looked like fighting. The artillery blazed away, and we had a regular slam battle."[26]

The Cavalry Trains

Cavalry in the two armies relied at first on the '41 Tactics, mostly an anonymous translation of French cavalry manuals, and then on Colonel Philip St. George Cooke's *Tactics.* In general, training of Southern cavalrymen, who were on the whole lifelong horsemen, was confined to instruction in military basics such as how to ride in coordinated attacks and skirmishes and how to use a saber. Little attention was paid to the school of the soldier.

Not so in the North, where cavalry troopers began their military training just like the infantry, learning to march and so on. Also, like the infantry, the horse soldiers learned how to load their carbines, but like the foot soldiers, they seldom had a chance at target practice.

Since most recruits had joined the cavalry because of its glamour, they found the school of the soldier unendingly boring. Their interest, however, picked up with the

Rebel Troopers

No Civil War unit was less disciplined than the Confederate cavalry, many of whose officers and men were Southern aristocrats who refused to recognize anyone as a superior, even higher-ranking officers. In the following account, reproduced in Stephen Z. Starr's *The Union Cavalry in the Civil War,* newly promoted Confederate Captain French faces this discipline problem.

[Captain French] found it an extremely difficult task to bring any of the men [of his command] into any sort of subjection to discipline. . . . [He] had given positive orders that no man should leave camp without permission. . . . The order . . . was hardly spoken before some of his men were gone and remained out all night. . . . In the morning . . .

French met one of them. . . . "Did you not hear my order last night?" asked the Captain. "Yes, but I don't mind orders when I want to go anywhere" was the answer, but it was scarcely given before the Captain's sabre came down on his head, and the man fell, badly hurt. This created great excitement in the company, and while most of them joined in a petition to the Captain to resign, some of them threatened him with personal violence; but when he heard of it, he came out among the men alone, and proposed to give any or all of them the satisfaction [that is, fight] they required, and awed by his fearless manner, all of them to a man submitted . . . and ever afterwards Capt. French's orders were law.

issuance of sabers and the beginning of sword drill. The recruits soon found that the saber was not only heavy but unwieldy. Indeed, some, like their Confederate counterparts, accidentally pricked themselves, their fellows, and their horses.

Mounted drill eventually followed, although unlike the Southern cavalry, Northern recruits generally had to first learn how to ride. A history of the 7th Indiana illustrates how poorly prepared the average Northern cavalry recruit was:

The horses . . . had never been exercised in drill. . . . The men were as green as the horses. Some of them never having been on a horse's back, did not know how to mount. . . . [Some] had difficulty maintaining their position in the saddle, and some in attempting to mount found themselves suddenly on the ground. . . . The sabres in being drawn made a great rattling and clatter. . . . This was more than [the horses] could bear. Some of them reared . . . , depositing their riders on the ground; . . . others darted over the commons, their riders . . . holding on with both hands to the horses' manes . . . , presenting pictures not in common with accomplished equestrianism [horsemanship].[27]

Many Northern recruits were afraid of these large, difficult-to-control animals, and not without reason, as troopers were thrown, dragged, and kicked by their steeds, resulting in bruises and broken bones. The recruits, however, made progress, and although few became expert horsemen, they eventually learned to stay in the saddle and fight as a unit.

The Life of a Company

Training did more than make soldiers and cavalry troopers out of recruits. It also created close bonds within many companies. These units were small enough to feel like a family, and like a family, they were often good or bad depending on the family's head, in this case the company commander, the captain.

The captain saw that his unit had what it needed: food, shelter, equipment, and weapons. He saw that they stayed fit and healthy. And, of course, he led the company into battle.

Additionally, the captain knew all his men, as well as something about their home lives, particularly if they had domestic problems, which he sometimes had to settle. He listened to the soldiers' complaints and administered punishment in minor matters, conducted religious services, oversaw burials, and wrote letters of condolence to the families of the dead.

The captain depended on his lieutenants, sergeants, and corporals to fashion the company into a single fighting unit by relaying and interpreting his commands to the unit's privates. And a good company always became a single unit, often seeming to think and act as one.

Civil War Discipline

Confederate and Union troops received their first taste of army discipline during training. For most volunteers, officers and men alike, obeying orders without question was an unpleasant novelty. These orders covered everything from what a soldier could eat and wear, to what he did during the day, to when and where he slept.

The volunteers hated these restrictions on what they saw as their basic freedoms guaranteed them as Americans or Confederates. As a consequence, most soldiers on both sides resisted their superiors' commands to varying degrees. One Union officer complained that no matter how long volunteer soldiers were trained, they would scratch and wiggle even when supposedly ordered to stand motionless

Good Conduct

Officers, particularly regular army, complained about the lack of discipline in both Federal and Confederate volunteer ranks. However, English journalist and observer Edward Dicey wrote that he was much impressed by the conduct of Union troops. His account appears in Commager's *The Blue and the Gray.*

> The rank and file of the American army is the most orderly I have ever seen. . . . There is less brutality about the Federal troops, and more respect for women, than amongst any soldiery . . . in the Old World [Europe].

> It once happened to me . . . to have to escort a party of ladies, after dark, across the long-chain bridge of Washington [D.C.]. . . . The whole bridge was crowded with a confused mass of Federal soldiers, who were halting there on their march southwards. . . . It was obvious many of them had drunk freely on breaking up their camp. . . . It was so dark, that no discipline could be maintained. . . . We had almost to grope our way through . . . the soldiers. . . . The number of gentlemen in our party was so small, we could have afforded little protection to the ladies . . . in case any insult had been

offered to them. . . . I can only say that, during the whole of that long passage, no remark whatever was addressed to us. The moment it was seen that there were ladies in our party, the soldiers got up from the planks, on which they were lying, to make way for us; and the songs (many of them loose [obscene] enough). . . were hushed immediately at our approach.

Federal troops are seen here at rest under the watchful eyes of their officers, who often complained about poor discipline.

during review. The Confederate general Joseph Johnston, a lifetime professional soldier, had nothing but contempt for the volunteers' lack of discipline.

As for the volunteers, as one Federal remarked, they could see no purpose to the "red-tape tomfoolery of the regular service," for "the boys recognized no superiors, except in the line of legitimate duty."[28] The Federal and Confederate enlisted men of the volunteer companies were often boyhood playmates of their officers, whom they had been calling by their first names until enlistment. In the South, some of the privates were actually richer and more socially prominent than their officers.

An additional sore point was the significant number of incompetent, drunken, or overbearing officers who had found their way into the service through political pull, social position, or wealth. The Union managed to rid itself of some of these men when it set up a screening board in 1861 to determine each officer's fitness to serve. In one midwestern regiment alone, seventeen officers were forced to resign.

Military Law

Even before training started, at their swearing in, all recruits were read the articles of war. These articles laid out the major points of military law and told soldiers that they had to obey orders from superiors. If they did not, they were guilty of insubordination. The articles also listed other acts deemed criminal, including treason, deser-

tion, mutiny, rape, theft, and murder. In theory, all of these crimes could result in a court-martial—that is, a trial by military court—and many were punishable by death. Some recruits were so frightened by the articles that they resigned on the spot.

Next to absent without leave, insubordination, and drunkenness, desertion was the major disciplinary problem for both Union and Confederate armies, particularly before a major campaign. It was easy for soldiers to simply leave, and there was virtually no way in nineteenth-century America to track down these men, particularly since the number of deserters ran into the thousands on both sides. Writer Jack Coggins notes that

> As accustomed as we are to the rules, regulations, and red tape of soldiering in the twentieth century, it seems incredible that thousands of men of both armies should wander off. . . . [Yet] it is safe to estimate that, given twenty thousand infantry to start with, a general would be lucky if, after two or three weeks . . . , he would be able to put sixteen thousand into the line of battle.[29]

Indeed, one Union general estimated that some 8,000 men and 250 officers deserted from the Army of the Potomac's I Corps before the Battle of Antietam.

Southern soldiers often left their units after a major battle and went home. These men believed that they had served the Confederacy, and now they were needed at home to bring in the crops or to earn money to feed their families.

Special Courts-Martial

Few offenses actually led to a court-martial, and even fewer to execution. In-

Soldiers guilty of minor offenses were assigned unpleasant tasks such as digging ditches (pictured) or filling in latrines.

deed, most offenders were never formally charged. Instead, the first sergeant of a company would keep a list of those found sitting on guard duty, drunk, stealing from other soldiers, or leaving camp without a pass. He would then assign these men to fill in latrines, bury dead horses, or perform any number of necessary but nasty tasks.

Still, courts-martial were common in both North and South. Those convened by regimental commanders were known as special courts-martial, which tried only noncapital crimes (not involving the death penalty) and enlisted men. Three officers sat in judgment; they could sentence a soldier to lose a month's pay or to spend thirty days in prison or at hard labor. If the man was a noncommissioned officer, the court could demote him.

Punishment Detail

Special courts-martial could also dispense shorter punishments, all of which were harsh and cruel by modern standards. A favorite of these courts was bucking and gagging. A thin log was thrust behind the knees and over the elbows of a gagged, guilty man. Then the man's hands were tied to his ankles so that he could not move. After several hours, sometimes a full

Mutiny

In August 1861, the 79th New York Regiment, known as the Highlanders, mutinied in the belief that they had been tricked into remaining in the army after the First Battle of Bull Run. This report of the mutiny by Captain William Lusk appears in *The Blue and the Gray*, edited by Henry Steele Commager.

> The mutiny commenced [began] in the morning by the men's refusing to strike [take down] their tents as commanded. . . . Col. Stevens repeated the orders, but they were silently and sullenly neglected. . . . Col. Stevens next sent to each company singly and read the articles of war, appending [adding] to them such remarks as would enforce in the men the danger of their course. . . .

> Soon a scene of the wildest confusion took place. The soldiers, throwing off all authority, presented the hideous . . . spectacle of a . . . drunken Helotry [mob of peasants]. . . . The Colonel ordered the officers to strike the tents themselves. This we did amid the jeers, the taunts, and the insults of an infuriated [angry] mob. . . . Everywhere we were threatened, and it became . . . necessary to show neither fear of the men, nor . . . to allow ourselves any act of violence which would precipitate [cause] bloodshed. . . .

> I was quite exhausted when a body of cavalry and a line of infantry appeared, coming toward us. . . . The mutineers . . . were surrounded, and . . . obeyed the orders issued, a death penalty being promised those who wavered. . . . The punishment awarded to the regiment . . . [was] the taking of the colors [regimental flag] and the disgrace from which we are suffering.

Union officers take away the colors of the 79th New York Infantry Regiment as punishment for mutiny.

day, the soldier was released, generally crying in great pain from cramps and unable to walk.

Other punishments included wearing a cannonball chained to a leg, having to march around the camp with a pack filled with rocks, or being made to stand on top of a barrel. Like bucking and gagging, such punishments lasted hours, sometimes a full day.

Cavalry units used all these punishments plus some special ones of their own. A trooper might be made to sit astride a

Carrying a log while chained to a cannonball, standing on a barrel, and bucking (not pictured) were some of the punishments issued for disobeying orders and other offenses.

log, to which legs and a head were fastened, making it look like a wooden horse. At the end of the punishment, the "rider" would dismount stiff and sore. Another cavalry punishment detail required carrying a saddle around the parade ground for several hours.

In artillery units, a common punishment was to tie a soldier spread-eagled on a wheel that was then lashed onto a gun carriage. The carriage was then driven over rough ground, inflicting a great deal of pain on the bound man as it bounced. Those who cried out in agony were gagged with a tied stick.

General Courts-Martial

More serious crimes, which included mutiny, rape, desertion, and murder, or crimes which involved an officer, were tried by general courts-martial. These courts had a board of five to thirteen examining offi-

cers, as well as an additional officer, called a judge-advocate, who tried the case and called witnesses.

Both Federal and Confederate general courts-martial handed down several hundred death sentences during the war. Although some of the convicted were hanged, most were executed by firing squad. Generally, the condemned was blindfolded, arms tied behind his back, and made to sit on his coffin facing a firing

Blindfolded and sitting on his casket, a condemned man is executed by a firing squad. Hanging was another method of execution.

squad of twelve men. After the volley, the presiding officer sometimes had to fire a final shot, the coup de grâce.

Another punishment handed down by general courts-martial was branding. A soldier found guilty of desertion had a *D* burned into his forehead, cheek, hand, or hip; a coward was branded with a *C* and a thief with a *T*. Sometimes permanent ink was used instead of a hot branding iron.

In addition to condemning a guilty soldier to death, a general court-martial could order a man be drummed out of the service. In front of gathered troops, the guilty man was stripped of buttons and rank insignia, shaved of his hair, and escorted out of camp to the tune of "The Rogues' March" in the North and "Yankee Doodle" in the South. General courts-martial could also send an offender to military prison, as happened to

sixty-three members of the 2nd Maine found guilty of mutiny.

Many soldiers resented these punishments, particularly the executions, which they were forced to watch. However, others considered the brutality necessary. A Confederate wrote that "these severe punishments seem necessary to preserve discipline," sentiments echoed by a Federal: "They . . . served their purpose. . . . The times were cruel, and men had been hardened to bear the suffering of other men without wincing."[30] For whatever reason—cruel punishments, better officers, seasoned men—disciplinary problems declined in the last two years of the war.

Discipline was only a part of the soldiers' and cavalry trooper's life. The Federal and Confederate volunteers had to adjust to living in army quarters and eating army food, as well as to the army's daily routine.

Chapter 4

In Camp

Routine was the word for camp life for both Federal and Confederate troops. Combat was one of the few breaks in this routine, which consisted in large part of drill, marching for the infantry and mounted exercises for the cavalry. As one soldier put it:

> The first thing in the morning is drill, then drill, then drill, then drill again. Then drill, drill, drill, a little more drill. Then drill and lastly drill. Between drills we drill and sometimes stop to eat a little and have roll call.[31]

The routine of drill was broken from time to time with free periods. During these periods, soldiers entertained themselves with talking; music, particularly singing; writing letters and keeping journals; and baseball and other games.

Reveille and the Day Begins

When troops in both Northern and Southern armies were not on the march or in

battle, they spent their days essentially the same way. They got up early, 5:00 A.M. in the summer and 6:00 A.M. in the winter. Drums for the infantry or bugles for the cavalry sounded reveille, and the soldier or cavalryman had fifteen minutes to wash and dress before assembly of the company or cavalry squadron and roll call. Anyone missing was put down for extra work or other punishment. The first sergeant read any special orders for the day, and then the infantry and artillery went to breakfast.

Before they could eat, however, the cavalry had to feed and groom their horses. Then, after washing up and breakfast, the men walked their horses to the nearest stream or pond so their mounts could drink.

Chores and Drill

For all units, no matter the service, camp chores such as chopping firewood and policing the grounds occupied the first part of the morning, as did sick call. During

The cavalry made sure that their livestock was cared for and fed before they ate. Here, a Union soldier takes his mule for a morning drink.

guard stood or rode sentry duty two out of every six hours for the next twenty-four.

Those not assigned to work parties or guard duty spent the rest of the morning drilling. These exercises, generally company or squadron drills but sometimes regimental, included marching and riding in formation as well as weapons practice.

Confederate cavalry units were not as given to drill as Union cavalry or, for that matter, Confederate infantry. Some Southern cavalry commanders, such as Nathan Bedford Forrest, thought such workouts a waste of time and a drain on men and horses. Others, however, like Jeb Stuart, drilled their troopers hard.

Day's End

Lunch, known as dinner, was called at noon by drums and bugles playing "Roast Beef." Following lunch was some free time and then more drill, with late afternoon devoted to tent inspection and a second watering of the cavalry's horses.

At 5:45 P.M. came retreat, which consisted of an inspection and a dress parade. Each soldier and cavalry trooper carefully checked to see that his weapons and buckles were polished, his belt and other leather items shined, and his uniform brushed. At retreat, officers read out or-

this time, each company or squadron's first sergeant gathered those men chosen for guard duty and turned them over to the regiment's corporal of the guard. Each ders, messages from army command, and court-martial results. Then the soldiers went to supper, except the cavalry, who first had to feed their horses.

After supper, a soldier or cavalry trooper who was not on guard or a work detail was free to talk, play cards, or get up a baseball game. At 8:30 P.M., he had to report to a final assembly and roll call known as tattoo.

A half-hour later taps sounded, and the enlisted men had to be in bed with lights out and no talking. Those caught breaking the curfew would find themselves slated for extra work. Although officers were supposed to obey lights out, many did not, for as Union private John Billings observed, "here, as elsewhere, rank interposed to shield culprits, . . . [and] officers . . . did get together, . . . making tenfold the disturbance ever caused by the . . . private after hours."[32]

Sunday and Reviews

Sunday was the only day of the week on which this routine varied. After breakfast, the privates of both companies and squadrons prepared for the formal regimental inspection. The regimental commander or his junior officers came to each unit's site, examining quarters, cooking areas, and grounds. In what was called knapsack drill, each man's effects were also inspected. The remainder of Sunday was free time, although in some units, particularly Confederate, attendance at religious services was mandatory.

The cavalry had less of a break than did the infantry and the artillery on Sunday. As on any other day, the horse soldiers had to feed and water their mounts twice a day. And, of course, guards from all units, no matter the service branch, had to be posted.

Another break in routine was the occasional brigade or division review. The men of each unit spruced themselves up and then marched or rode past the brigade or division commander and his staff. Then the troops demonstrated a variety of marching or riding maneuvers.

Federal troops attend a religious service at a camp chapel. In Confederate camps, church attendance was mandatory.

Reviews were generally ordered when important visitors, such as senior Federal or Confederate army officers or government officials, were present in camp. Sometimes, these events were a way of boosting morale, as Jeb Stuart discovered. His Confederate cavalry brigade put on a series of very elaborate reviews, in which the unit's "horses were groomed to a brilliant sheen, boots and sabers polished, [and] dress uniforms exhibited."[33] Stuart's men would then do riding tricks and stage mock battles, all of which went down well with both participants and observers.

Living in Tents

No matter what the day, except when in battle, three things were uppermost in the average Northern or Southern soldier's or cavalry trooper's mind: sleep,

---

Dog Tents

Dog, or pup, tents, made from three shelter halves, became the most common tenting in both armies after 1862. In his journal, *Soldiering: The Civil War Diary of Rice C. Bull, 123rd New York Volunteer Infantry*, Bull describes his makeshift shelter.

> Each man was issued a tent cloth. . . . Usually three men would occupy a tent as . . . [their] three cloths could be so arranged as to enclose . . . the three sides of a tent, in which they could lie. These tents were to be used chiefly for sleeping, as one could barely sit erect at the highest place in the center. They were far from comfortable living quarters. Yet they were the only kind of shelter we could have in the field during our term of service. For three years this thin cloth would be our cover from wind, storm and cold. . . . The head of our bed was at the back where we used our knapsacks for pillows. For our beds we would first spread our rubber blankets, on top of which we placed one woolen blanket, for covering we used two other blankets. In fair weather we

stacked our guns in the street but when it was stormy took them into the tent to keep them dry. . . . In wet, cold times [the tents] were anything but satisfactory. They would shed water when it came gently but if the storm was heavy the rain would come through, at first like damp mist and when the cloth was well soaked would run through in big drops like a leaking roof.

Their dog tents set up, these soldiers are catching up with the latest news.

---

food, and free time. Federal and Confederate troops slept in tents, except during the winter. For the first year of the war, the standard issue was the Sibley, a large conical, or bell-shaped, tent some twelve feet in height. Its seven square feet of floor space housed four easily, but often as many as twenty men were forced to share a Sibley. Sleeping in a circle with their feet pointed toward the center, the soldiers were so crowded that, as one Union soldier observed, "if one wanted to turn over . . . , he would yell out the order to 'flop' and all would go together." Few soldiers liked the Sibley, with one Confederate calling them "those abominations, those breeders of disease."[34]

Because they were so large and heavy, the Sibley tents were hard to transport, and their use was discontinued in 1862. Replacing them was the shelter half. Nothing more than a sheet of canvas six feet by four, three shelter halves were fastened together to form a wedge with one open end that barely accommodated three men. The resulting tent was known as a dog or pup tent because the soldiers joked only a small dog could live in one.

Sleeping in a dog tent during rain was very uncomfortable, for like all Civil War tents, water eventually soaked through the canvas and dripped onto the occupants. Additionally, wind and rain often blew in the open end, which some soldiers partially blocked off by hanging coats and blankets. At the height of summer, these tents were stifling hot; some soldiers pitched their shelter tents so that the sides did not meet the ground, allowing for air circulation.

Shebangs and Log Cabins

Tents were much more common among the Federals than among the shortage-plagued Confederates. Some Southern soldiers slept in pairs sandwiched between a blanket on the ground and another on top. Others cobbled together a hut called a shebang, which could sleep four. The shebang could be thrown together in a day and had a wood frame hung with pieces of thin boards, canvas, blankets, bushes, or whatever else was at hand.

During the winter when combat generally ground to a halt because of cold, rain, and snow, Federals and Confederates alike set up more permanent sleeping quarters. Several men would get together and build a little log cabin, the logs placed either horizontally, one atop the other, or vertically like a fence. The roof was made of boards, thatch, or fastened-together shelter halves. The men plastered mud between the logs to stop drafts and to trap heat. Lastly, the cabin owners used more logs to build a fireplace, sometimes even with a chimney. The fanciest of the cabins had interior walls, creating rooms.

Signs and Beds

Over the entrance of tents and cabins were crudely lettered boards announcing that one was entering Hawkin's Happy Family, Fifth Avenue Hotel, Social Circle, Old Abe's Parlor, Chateau de Salt Junk,

Union soldiers at work in front of their winter sleeping quarters, which they have named "Pine Cottage."

or whatever other whimsical name struck the occupants' fancy. The inside could be neat, cozy, or messy, although during rains, particularly in tents, all interiors became wet and muddy.

The beds that soldiers and cavalry troopers used were as varied as the men themselves. One Federal soldier wrote:

A. spreads his blanket upon his tent floor . . . and uses his boots for a pillow; B. nails up a long narrow box, strongly suggestive of that unpleasant, black looking shell [coffin], in which we all sleep our last slumber; another makes his couch of small cedar . . . twigs, carefully laid one upon the other; while he who is more fastidious [picky], drives into the ground four forked sticks, rests upon them two slender poles, to which a . . . number of barrel staves are fastened cross ways, and spreading his blankets, enjoys a . . . bed as luxurious as any that crowd the warehouses back home.[35]

Mess Mates

Tent and cabin mates and their neighbors commonly grouped themselves in an informal arrangement known as a mess. The members of a mess ate together. Collectively, they drew several days' rations at a time and, because neither Confederate nor Federal ranks included cooks, in most messes each soldier did his own cooking.

Mess mates clustered together because they were lifelong friends or because they had similar tastes and interests. They sometimes gave their group a name and each other nicknames. Thus, one mess in the 82nd Illinois became the Hyenas, with members being called Elephant, Bulldog Clipper, Greyhound, Weasel, and Tiger, among others.

Rations

It was no great feat for the average Civil War soldier or cavalry trooper to cook for himself. Rations were simple and easy to prepare. Both sides ate mostly the same kinds of food, although the Confederate army generally issued smaller portions and more often ran short. In camp, the troops ate bread, salt pork or bacon, beans, dried potatoes, dried vegetables, coffee, sugar, salt, and vinegar. Occasionally, cattle were delivered to a unit for butchering.

Salt pork or bacon was fried in a skillet, often heavy with grease, or skewered on a bayonet or sharp stick and held over a fire. Vegetables came in a small, pressed block that was cooked in boiling water, as were beans and potatoes.

In general, the rations on both sides were terrible, particularly meat, which was frequently rotten and full of maggots.

Salted meat was so full of salt that it was sometimes inedible even after having been soaked in fresh water for hours. Pickled beef was often rancid. Even freshly butchered meat could not be trusted: Soldiers reported having seen slabs of newly cut meat left hanging so long that they became covered in flies, while others watched butchers throw the meat into the mud and dung of slaughtering pens.

Hardtack and Cornbread

The bread supplied to both sides also had its problems. Normally, Union troops dined on a hard bread, more like a large, thick cracker, called hardtack. Hardtack was often moldy and filled with weevils or maggots, leading to its being called worm castles. The soldiers would sometimes crumble it into a cup of boiling coffee and skim the weevils off as they floated to the surface. Another favorite way of cooking the crackers was to fry them in pork grease to make a dish called skillygalee.

Hardtack was tough chewing, and legends grew up around it. Soldiers claimed that their teeth hurt for days after first eating it. Others said that even soaking it in coffee for six weeks would not soften it. Crates of hardtack bore the mark "B.C.," for brigade commissary, but the soldiers joked that it was the date of its manufacture.

Southern soldiers ate mostly cornbread, made from a coarse grain that produced a rubbery bread. Like hardtack, military cornbread produced its share of myths. Soldiers claimed that it could be

Hardtack

In *Hardtack and Coffee*, John D. Billings reminisces about that Union army staple, hardtack.

What was hardtack? It was a plain flour-and-water biscuit. . . . When they were poor and fit objects for the soldiers' wrath, it was due to one of three conditions. First, they may have been so hard that they could not be bitten; it then required a very strong blow of the fist to break them. . . .

The second condition was when they were mouldy or wet. . . . I think this condition was often due to their having been boxed up too soon after baking. It certainly was frequently due to exposure to the weather. . . .

The third condition was when from storage they had become infested with maggots and weevils. These weevils were, in my experience, more abundant than the maggots. They were a little slim, brown bug an eighth of an inch in length . . . , having the ability to completely riddle the hardtack. I believe they never interfered with the hardest variety. . . .

But hardtack was not so bad an article of food, even when traversed [crossed] by insects. . . . Eaten in the dark, no one could tell the difference between it and hardtack that was untenanted. . . .

There were a score [twenty] ways adopted to make this simple *flour tile* more edible. . . . [They were] crumbled in coffee. . . . Probably more were eaten in this way than in any other. . . . Some . . . crumbed them in soups. . . . Some crumbed them in cold water, then fried the crumbs in the juice and fat of meat. . . . Some liked them toasted.

Union army cooks stand outside a supply tent filled with hardtack, the oftentimes inedible biscuits made out of flour and water.

stretched into ropes or formed into balls that bounced.

Cornbread was often made into cakes, called slapjacks, which were cooked over an open fire. Confederate soldiers also used it to make a dish called cush or slosh. Into a skillet would go all the meat that a mess had. Then grease, water, and cornbread were added and cooked until the mixture had thickened up. Cush was an easy meal to make, if not a particularly digestible one.

Coffee

If the food was bad, the coffee was generally good, at least in the North. Union soldiers loved coffee, and each one carried a bag of coffee beans, which he crushed with his rifle butt. During any free time Federals turned to building fires and brewing coffee. It "was the mainstay," observed one northern soldier, and "without it was misery indeed." A fellow Federal claimed that, to a soldier, coffee was "considered to him indispensable . . . as the air he breathes."[36]

Consequently, the Union army made sure that even if no other rations were available, coffee was. The army even experimented with instant coffee, which was a mixture of coffee, milk, and sugar. One teaspoon of this coffee essence, as it was called, made a cup of coffee. However, the soldiers did not like it, and the army stopped issuing it.

Confederate soldiers also liked coffee, but it was in short supply during the war because of the blockade. Its presence usually meant troops had taken coffee beans from dead or captured Federals. Mostly, Southern soldiers made do with coffee substitutes made from peanuts, potatoes, peas, corn, or rye.

Tobacco

In addition to coffee, tobacco was one of the great pleasures of a soldier's or cavalry trooper's life. It was smoked, chewed, and snorted with relish, particularly among Southerners, who ranked it in importance just behind food.

Although the men of both sides used tobacco, Confederate use was much greater since, being a major Southern cash crop, tobacco was so much more readily available in the South than in the North. Federal soldiers noted that tobacco was so common that even women chewed and smoked it, as did some children, a practice almost unheard of in the Union.

However, as the fighting dragged on, the supply of Southern tobacco dwindled, as tobacco fields were occupied by Union troops or left unplanted because of a shortage of farmers. Confederate soldiers complained bitterly of the rising cost of tobacco and the increasing difficulty of obtaining it. More than one Southern general wrote Richmond demanding that his troops be given first shot at available tobacco supplies. The plant eventually became an important form of barter among Southern soldiers.

Readin' and Writin'

Coffee drinking and tobacco use often accompanied off-duty activities. It was during free moments that soldiers wrote letters home and, more importantly, read and reread letters from home. They also recorded their day-to-day experiences in the diaries and journals that remain among the best sources of what Federal and Confederate army life was really like.

Getting Out the Vote

In the following letter, reprinted in *The Blue and the Gray,* edited by Henry Steele Commager, Federal officer George Breck explains how soldiers voted in the 1864 presidential election, which pitted Republican incumbent Abraham Lincoln against Democrat and Union general George McClellan.

I have been very, very busy . . . with company matters, and with politics also. Last week was devoted . . . to the polling of votes from the company. . . . Quite a strong vote was cast for Lincoln in consequence of a number of new recruits, between thirty and forty, having joined . . . very recently . . . from . . . [a] strong Republican district. . . . Nearly all the old men [veteran soldiers] voted for McClellan. I shall send my vote home by Lieut. Anderson to give to Father to poll [cast]. Quite a form has to be gone through by New York soldiers who vote, giving power of attorney to some legal voter where they reside to cast their vote for them, taking an oath that they are legal voters, etc. all of which requires a great deal of writing. The affidavits [oaths] are administered by some commanding officer, and I being such, I have administered something in the neighborhood of 500 oaths. . . Such . . . favoritism . . . as has been shown . . . Lincoln, by many officers in the army, . . . you little imagine. Hundreds of soldiers have been literally proscribed [forbidden] from voting for McClellan by their officers, and they have been obliged to get McClellan ballots from other sources and to get other officers to administer the necessary oath to them.

Although Union soldiers had a higher literacy rate than Confederates, reading was an important diversion for troops in both camps. Reading material was frequently scarce, and consequently, the troops would read anything. Favorites were newspapers, particularly the illustrated, or picture, papers. Some Union and Confederate regiments published their own newspapers, either using portable printing presses or writing them out by hand. During the course of the war, some two hundred of these homemade papers circulated among the two armies, some lasting only one or two issues, others several months. They bore such titles as *Buck and Ball, Camp Kettle, Unconditional S. Grant,* and *Pioneer Banner.*

Books were also prized, and the works of Milton, Swift, and Cooper, among many others, fueled literary discussion groups. Even more popular were Beadle's Dime Novels, sensational thrillers often about frontiersmen and Indian fighting. Thousands of these flooded army camps North and South. Regardless, it was the Bible that was the most widely read book among Federals and Confederates.

Racing, Snowballs, and Baseball

Civil War soldiers also formed debating clubs and amateur theatrical productions to pass the time. Tall-tale spinning was always popular, as were general bull sessions. Woodcarving of everything from pipes to chess pieces occupied many a soldier's free hours. And in all units could be found checker and chess players.

Sports from wrestling to footraces to football were also popular among Northern and Southern troops. Cavalry units, North and South, enjoyed horse racing; Southerners added spice to their contests by conducting them within firing range of Union sentries. Giant snowball fights between regimental companies during the winter were also a favorite activity of Federals and Confederates alike.

The most popular sport, however, was baseball, and pickup games were common in both armies during warm months. Two versions of the game existed during the war. One resembled the modern game, with a four-base diamond and three outs per inning. The other had two bases, one out per inning, and a rule that after hitting the ball, the batter, known as the striker, could keep running between bases until struck by a thrown ball. Each circuit of the bases was a scoring point, and consequently scores in this baseball were often high; one game reportedly ended with a score of 66 to 20.

Gambling and Drinking

Betting on the outcome of baseball games, wrestling matches, and horse races was widespread in both armies. When no other contest offered itself, soldiers would place bets on racing lice. Each soldier would place a single louse on his tin plate, and the first louse to move off the plate was the winner. Soldiers of the 1st Tennessee Regiment discovered that Private Sam Watkins had fixed the winning streak of his louse by secretly heating his plate before the race.

Card games such as poker, twenty-one,

faro, euchre, and whist went on in every camp, and it was a rare card game that was not played for stakes. A particularly popular form of gambling was a dice and board game called chuck-a-luck, whose players bet on a combination of numbers showing on three dice dropped through a funnel. In one Confederate regiment, a private relieved a number of his fellows of their recently received back pay with chuck-a-luck.

Besides gambling, soldiers sought relief from army life in drinking. Although gambling and drinking were violations of Federal and Confederate regulations, both were difficult to control or prevent. In part, this difficulty arose from the sheer prevalence of these activities in some units. One Union cavalry trooper wrote his family that "our camp is infested more or less with gambling . . . [and] drunkenness."[37] Moreover, officers who were supposed to enforce antialcohol and antigambling regulations were themselves drinkers and gamblers.

The popularity of gambling and drinking notwithstanding, the most common form of diversion in the Northern and Southern armies was music. Many soldiers on both sides carried and played musical instruments, and many companies and regiments had bands. One Confederate brigade routinely woke to a band concert.

The youngest members of these bands, and indeed of either army, were the drummer boys. They ranged in age from nine to the early teens and, despite their name, were just as likely to play the bugle or fife as the drums. In some cases, drummer boys

This drummer boy served with the Union's 78th Regiment. Sometimes as young as nine years old, drummer boys often became the stuff of legend.

counts the brave death of Henry Burke of the 58th Ohio. However, the only Henry Burke on the regiment's rolls was a private who enlisted two years after the Battle of Shiloh. A Henry Burke on the Shiloh memorial was added, it turns out, after Hays's song became a hit.

Still, some drummer boys did have heroic adventures. Drummer boy Charley Common, after losing his drum, grabbed a rifle and fought alongside the 52nd Ohio at Perryville. And Orion P. Howe of the 55th Illinois was wounded while carrying messages during the siege of Vicksburg.

John L. Clem was the most famous drummer boy of the war. As a ten-year-old with the 22nd Michigan, Clem's drum was smashed by a shell at Shiloh. Clem was unhurt and became known thereafter as Shiloh Johnny. Although still technically a drummer boy, Johnny fought at Chickamauga, where, when ordered to surrender by a Confederate colonel, the young boy shot the man off his horse. After the war, Clem tried unsuccessfully to enter West Point. Finally, with the help of President Ulysses S. Grant, he became a second lieutenant in the army, from which he retired in 1916 as a major general.

The Soldiers Sing

With or without bands or musical instruments, the Civil War soldier and cavalryman sang. Southern and Northern troops sang to entertain themselves, to relieve homesickness and loneliness, and to raise their spirits before a battle. They also sang

were officially attached to a company; in others, they were unofficial members, almost mascots of companies and regiments.

These young boys often became the stuff of legend. Will S. Hays's popular song "Drummer Boy of Shiloh" supposedly reas they marched, the cadence of the songs helping keep them in step.

Many songs of the period were favorites of Federal and Confederate troops alike. Indeed, the unofficial national anthem of the Confederacy, "Dixie," had been written two years before the war by Dan Emmett of Ohio. Jefferson Davis had "Dixie" played at his inauguration, and Abraham Lincoln had it played when news of Robert E. Lee's surrender reached Washington, D.C.

The most popular song among the troops was "Home Sweet Home." Other favorites included "John Brown's Body," "Maryland, My Maryland," "When Johnny Comes Marching Home," and hymns such as "Old Hundred," "Amazing Grace," and "Rock of Ages."

Publishers of the North and South did a booming business in sheet music and songbooks of soldier songs. Several collections, including *Songs of the South, General Lee Songster, Beadle's Dime Union Song Book,*

Songs of the War

Civil War soldiers marched to many tunes, but none was more popular with Federals than "John Brown's Body," with its references to the executed abolitionist, and only "Dixie" was more popular with Confederates than "The Bonnie Blue Flag," which hailed the first single-starred flag of the Confederacy. The lyrics of both songs are reproduced in *The Blue and the Gray*, edited by Henry Steele Commager.

John Brown's Body

John Brown's body lies a-mould'ring in the
    grave,
John Brown's body lies a-mould'ring in the
    grave,
John Brown's body lies a-mould'ring in the
    grave,
    His soul is marching on.

    Chorus: Glory! Glory Hallelujah!
        Glory! Glory Hallelujah!
        Glory! Glory Hallelujah!
        His soul is marching on.

He's gone to be a soldier in the army of the
    Lord!
    His soul is marching on.—Chorus

Now for the Union let's give three rousing
    cheers.
    As we go marching on.

    Hip, hip, hip, hip, hurrah!—Chorus

* * * * * *

The Bonnie Blue Flag

We are a band of brothers, and natives to the
    soil,
Fighting for the property we gained by honest toil;
And when our rights were threatened, the cry
    rose near and far:
Hurrah for the bonnie Blue Flag that bears a
    single star!
    Hurrah! Hurrah! for the bonnie Blue Flag
    That bears a single star!

As long as the Union was faithful to her trust,
Like friends and like brothers, kind were we
    and just;
But now when Northern treachery attempts
    our rights to mar,
We hoist on high the bonnie Blue Flag that
    bears a single star. . . .

and *Yankee Doodle Songster,* were marketed directly to the troops. Even today, much of this music is still played and sung.

The most famous song of the Civil War was "The Battle Hymn of the Republic," written by Julia Ward Howe to the tune of "John Brown's Body." Howe's lyrics were first published in the *Atlantic Monthly* as a poem in February 1862, where they were quickly picked up by Federal troops. During the Battle of Gettysburg, Union inmates in Libby Prison in Richmond, Virginia, were told by their jailers that the Confederacy had just won a great victory. They were overjoyed when an African American slave who brought them their food told them that the jailers were lying. Some of the prisoners began singing "The Battle Hymn of the Republic," all joining in on the chorus, "Glory, glory, hallelujah," and making the prison ring with the song.

Members of a Union regimental band pose with their instruments. On one occasion, a Federal band played songs requested by Confederates who were close by.

Getting Together

Northern and Southern soldiers sometimes sang competitively. A Confederate lieutenant wrote his family that "we are on one side of the Rappahannock [River], the Enemy on the other. . . . Our boys will sing a Southern song. The Yankees will reply by singing the same tune to Yankee words."[38]

At one point, while still camped across the Rappahannock from the Federals, Confederates sat on the riverbank and listened to a concert given by a Union regimental band. From time to time, a Southern soldier yelled a request across the waters, and the Northern band played it.

On occasion, unofficial truces would be called, and the two sides would actually get together to sing, to talk, or share a meal and coffee. Such affairs were an extension of the thousands of times that Federal and Confederate sentries, posted near each other, would share tobacco, food, coffee, and news. Historian James Robertson writes:

[These] opposing forces spoke the same language; they had the same likes and dislikes, the same backgrounds and cultures, the same roots in America's soil. . . . Kinfolk fighting on opposite

During a truce, Union and Confederate soldiers trade coffee and tobacco.

sides promoted fraternization [associating]. So did . . . camp boredom, and war weariness as the struggle dragged on. . . . Common desires among soldiers for Northern coffee and Southern tobacco contributed to friendly relations. And because the Civil War . . . [had] much idle time between contests, . . . anger [was] difficult to sustain. . . [and] ample opportunity . . . existed to be-

come acquainted with counterparts across a field or . . . a river.[39]

However, such friendly gatherings of Confederates and Federals were short-lived. Soon enough came the orders to return to war, and the soldiers and cavalry set off to the next battlefield and a very different sort of meeting.

Chapter 5

On the March

Historian Bell Irvin Wiley writes that "the Civil War was to a large extent a war of movement. A normal prelude to a battle was a march."[40] Sometimes, this movement was accomplished by loading troops onto trains or boats, but more commonly, the soldiers walked and the cavalry rode, both activities covered by the word *march*. When Lee invaded Pennsylvania in the summer of 1863, he and his entire army—infantry, cavalry, and artillery— marched all the way from Northern Virginia to Gettysburg. The opposing Army of the Potomac covered the same distance, also on foot and horse. Getting to battle was thus a slow, tiring, muscle-aching business.

Orders and Preparations

For both Federals and Confederates, a march began at sunset with company and cavalry squadron commanders reporting to regimental headquarters. There the colonel would order them to prepare their men to leave, normally around 6:00 A.M. the next day.

Union company and cavalry squadron commanders wait for their orders regarding an upcoming march.

The captains then gathered their units and inspected weapons, uniforms, equipment, and, in the cavalry, horses and tack. The commanders also oversaw the distribution of ammunition, confirming that each soldier or cavalry trooper had at least sixty rounds. At the same time, lieutenants and sergeants secured enough rations so that each company or squadron member had three days' worth of provisions, consisting of salt pork, sugar, and salt. Union troops also received coffee and hardtack; Confederates packed corn meal. The food that needed cooking was prepared that evening.

All of these arrangements took about an hour. From then until bedtime, the soldiers discarded, often burning, any extra gear that they did not want to carry. The unit bedded down at its usual time.

Guards duty was drawn among those men assigned light duty because of wounds or illness. Often these light-duty soldiers would not be joining the regiment on the march or, if accompanying the unit, would not be in the coming fight. Thus, all those who were fit for combat were allowed a full night's sleep.

Striking Camp

Well before sunrise, the troops were up. First to rise were the cavalry. "In the morning, if the cavalry are to move at the same hour [as] the infantry," wrote one Union horse soldier, "they must have reveille an hour earlier than the infantry to have time to feed, groom and saddle their horses."[41]

After breakfast, the men struck their tents. If they were leaving a winter camp, they set fire to the log cabins, leaving no dwellings for enemy use but spoiling the camp for friendly units as well. As the war progressed, some regiments abandoned the policy: As Union private Frank Wilkeson was told by his veteran companions, "Leave things as they are. . . . We may want them before snow flies."[42]

After roll and sick call, each man received his three days' of rations and then checked to be sure he had all his equipment, particularly bedroll and ammunition. Soldiers filled their canteens because most commanders were like Stonewall Jackson, who ordered that no one stop to drink while on the march.

The troops assembled in the standard infantry and cavalry marching order, a column, four abreast. Their route for the day, as well as for every other day of the march, had already been planned. Predetermined also were camp, or bivouac, sites for that night and other nights. The regiment's colonel and his staff, took their places at the head of the column, gave the command to march, and the unit moved out.

Like a long parade, the regimental column snaked along mostly narrow, unpaved dirt roads. If the march involved an entire army group, such as the Army of the Potomac or the Army of Northern Virginia, the column was surrounded by other regiments of its brigade, which were in turn part of the division and corps, all on the move in a miles-long stream of men and wagons.

Stepping Out

Found in Francis A. Lord's *They Fought for the Union*, the following firsthand account of the 13th New Hampshire Infantry's marching preparations could describe those of any unit in either the Federal or Confederate army at any time during the war.

The regiment is called at 4 A.M. The roll is called. At the Surgeon's call or previously it is determined what men are able to march, and what men not. . . . Breakfast [is] eaten, the cooked rations distributed, and informal inspection made of every man and his belongings, blankets are rolled, each man's blanket in a long roll, the ends of the roll brought together and tied, forming a sort of 'horse-collar,' all is made ready. . . .

The drums beat a quick assembly, the men fall into line along their musket stacks, the roll is again called. The colors [regimental flag] are brought out, . . . companies take their arms, . . . and the line is formed. . . .

When all is ready the Colonel takes command, gives the order to march, places himself with staff at the head of the column, and at the quick step of a lively march played on fife and drum, or by the band, the command [regiment]

moves out of the camp in column of four, . . . guns on the shoulder, each man with his roll of blankets thrown diagonally across his shoulders, every . . . canteen . . . and cartridgebox is full. . . . Soon the music ceases, the route-step is taken, . . . and the jaunty, joking, merry, laughing host [regiment] passes out of sight—to fell or to fall.

A regiment, complete with a marching band, advances out of its camp.

The column, whether a regiment or an army corps, contained a mix of infantry companies, cavalry squadrons, long lines of mule-drawn ammunition and supply wagons, and the artillery, mounted or riding their guns. Strung out for miles behind the main column were the stragglers: new recruits who were quickly exhausted and fell behind; still recovering ill and injured soldiers; and men with blistered feet or broken-down boots who just could not keep up the pace.

Trudging with the Infantry

The marching infantry soon dropped into route step; that is, walking as they pleased and carrying their rifles as they liked. Because the average infantry pace was two and one-half miles an hour, the walking soldiers had to scramble from time to time to the sides of the road to avoid the faster-moving cavalry, supply wagons, and artillery. The pace, however, was never steady. During the course of a day, as flats turned into hills or vice versa, or as wagons broke down, the infantry moved sometimes at a crawl, sometimes at a trot, and at times halted altogether.

At first there would be talk and laughter, even some singing, but before long the troops would fall silent as rifle and equipment grew heavy. As the day passed, the men wearied, although ten-minute breaks on the hour and sixty to seventy minutes' rest for lunch helped.

On the whole, the march was a hot, thirsty trudge, for as Robertson notes, "oppressive heat and stifling humidity prevailed during most of the months in the field. Flies and mosquitoes swarmed at every moment."[43] Clouds of dust kicked up by thousands of men and hundreds of horses and mules made things worse. The dust worked its way into mouths, eyes, and noses and cut visibility to a few yards.

Horse-drawn artillery makes its way over easy terrain. Often conditions were much worse, with rain, mud, or snow adding to the discomfort.

If it had recently rained, the roads were mud, and the entire column risked getting stuck on the march. Of such mud in Virginia and its consequences, Union soldier Rice B. Bull wrote:

We did not start until after ten o'clock [in the morning], as it was next to impossible to move the trains [of wagons] and artillery, the roads were in such wretched condition. There was no bottom to the mud which was sticky, red clay. . . . We could make no headway; it became a quagmire [swamp] blocked by stalled wagons and artillery that settled into the mud up to their wheel hubs, and the mules could not move them.[44]

However, nothing—neither heat, dust, rain, nor mud—was worse for walking men than foot problems. Blistered feet made an unrelieved torture of the hours of march. The feet of one Federal sergeant were rubbed so raw by his ill-fitting shoes that they became swollen, blistered, and infected. When he removed his shoes, he found that blood and pus had cemented sock to skin, and when he walked, the scabs on his feet cut like knives into his flesh.

To Scout and Harass

Riding in front, to the sides, and to the rear of the column were units of the cavalry. In an age without airplanes or spy satellites, cavalry was the only way generals could get fast, detailed reports on their enemy's movements. Army commanders also depended on their horse soldiers to screen them from the spying eyes of enemy cavalry. Additionally, the mounted soldiers made fast raids against the opposing army. On both sides, cavalry destroyed whatever supplies they could, although Confederates attempted to capture goods whenever possible.

At the beginning of the war, Confederate cavalry was far superior at these tasks than the Federals. However, by the war's midpoint in 1863, the Union horse soldiers' training and experience had made them the equal of Confederate units, and by war's end, the Northern troopers formed the better cavalry.

Often cavalry operations could take the mounted units far from the main body of the marching army. This separation could be dangerous. While advancing into Pennsylvania, Robert E. Lee lost touch with his cavalry under the command of Jeb Stuart. Consequently, Lee had no idea where the Army of the Potomac was or what it was doing. Thus, the Southern commander, whose string of victories owed much to his ability to pick the battlefield, had to wait until accident brought the two forces together at Gettysburg, a place definitely not of his choosing and the site of his Army of Northern Virginia's first major defeat.

Friendly Territory, Enemy Territory

Despite the occasional Southern thrust into Northern territory, such as Lee's invasion of Pennsylvania, most Civil War

Hard Riding

Cavalrymen rode instead of walked on campaign, but that advantage did not mean their life was a comfortable one. In the following two narratives, found in Stephen Z. Starr's *The Union Cavalry in the Civil War,* one regiment of Union horse soldiers rides for thirty hours without a break and another contends with foul weather.

[Some troopers] slept in their saddles, either leaning forward . . . or sitting quite erect, with an occasional bow forward or to the right or left, . . . like the careening [swaying] of a drunken man. . . . Sometimes a fast-walking horse in one of the rear companies will bear his sleeping lord quietly along . . . until the poor fellow is awakened, and finds himself just passing by the colonel and his staff at the head of the column.

* * * * * *

The boys waked up in good spirits and . . . [were] soon on the move. Shortly after starting, a mixed storm commenced—drizzle and rain, then rain and drizzle, drizzle and snow, and then snow; and the marching was made more uncomfortable by the condition of the roads, which fast grew muddy and rough. . . . A few miles farther on [we were] ordered to dismount and go into camp [make camp]. But 'go into camp' was a mere form of words. The horses were hitched up [tied down], and that is about all that was done. . . . The wagons were five miles away, stuck in the mud . . . ; consequently the regiment was without rations, . . . tents, axes, [and] cooking utensils. . . . The next day it still stormed, the air was colder, the mud was deeper.

weather, dust, mud, and thirst as Union soldiers, operated in home territory, which many of them knew intimately and in which most inhabitants were Confederate supporters. Southern troops, therefore, normally had only the Union army to worry about.

Not so the Federals, who found themselves moving cautiously through a foreign land, full of enemies both military and civilian. The Northern troops were surrounded by people who wanted to trick, capture, or kill them.

Aside from the Confederate military, the Federals' greatest danger came from guerrilla bands. Rice Bull reported that "the [Virginia] country is filled with guerrillas who were capturing and shooting any of our boys that had wandered [off]."[45]

One of the most successful Southern guerrillas was John Singleton Mosby. An officer in the Confederate cavalry, Mosby led a group of partisan rangers who, although technically soldiers, operated outside army discipline or regulations. Mosby, whose stealth earned him the name Gray Ghost, and his rangers attacked and captured Federal wagon trains and isolated Union outposts, as well as destroyed Union lines of communication.

It would be overstating the case to say that all Southern civilians were enthusiastic Confederates. Many were lukewarm at best, particularly when faced with armed Northern soldiers and cavalry. Additionally, regions of the South, such as east Tennessee, had not favored secession,

campaigning took place within the Confederacy. Thus, marching Southern troops, although just as stressed by and many people in these areas approved of and supported the Northern cause and the Northern soldier.

Foragers and Looters

Both armies were guilty of acts that angered friend and foe alike. Most notable among these offenses were foraging and looting. Foraging was the taking, rarely with payment, of goods from civilians. The object of most foraging was food, since both armies often lived off the land when campaigning. The Confederates did so because they were ever short of rations. The Federals resorted to foraging because their long supply lines into the South were regularly disrupted by Confederate cavalry and guerrillas.

Mosby's Guerrillas

John Munson was a member of John Singleton Mosby's band of Southern guerrillas. In the following excerpt from Commager's *The Blue and the Gray*, Munson gives an insider's view of Mosby's band.

> The life led by Mosby's men was entirely different from that of any other body of soldiers during the war. His men had no camps nor fixed quarters, and never slept in tents. They did not even know anything about pitching a tent. The idea of making coffee, frying bacon, or soaking hardtack was never entertained [considered]. When we wanted to eat we stopped at a friendly farm house, or went into some little town and bought what we wanted. Every man in the Command had some special farm he could call his home. . . .
>
> As a Command we had no knowledge of the first principles of cavalry drill, and could not be formed in a straight line had there been any need for our doing so. We did not know the bugle calls, and very rarely had roll-call. . . .
>
> 'Something gray' was the one requisite of our dress and the cost of it mattered little. . . . Some of the Command were extremely fastidious [fussy] in the manner of dress and affected gold braid, buff trimmings, and ostrich plumes in their hats. . . . At all times, whether things went well or ill, the Guerrillas were . . . blithe [cheerful] in the face of danger, full of song and story, indifferent to the events of tomorrow, and keyed up to a high pitch of anticipation.

John Singleton Mosby led a group of Southern guerrillas.

Confederate cavalrymen loot the town of New Windsor, Maryland, in 1864. Mounted units had more opportunities for plundering than foot soldiers.

large pieces of furniture, they destroyed. Additionally, they used wooden furnishings and fencing for firewood.

The Cavalry Helps Itself

The cavalry were the greatest looters in both armies. Their speed and mobility allowed them to cover greater distances and to carry away larger amounts of loot than the infantry. Further, mounted units operated far more independently than did infantry and, therefore, had far more opportunity to pillage.

Because Confederate cavalry operated mostly in the South, its chief targets were fellow Southerners. Z. B. Vance, the governor of North Carolina, wrote the Confederate secretary of war that "If God Almighty had yet in store another plague worse than all the others which he intended to have let loose on the Egyptians . . . it must have been a regiment or so of . . . half-disciplined Confederate cavalry."[46]

Charles Francis Adams, a member of the 1st Massachusetts Cavalry, voiced a similar sentiment about Northern cavalry. In a letter home, he observed:

Looting was common in those areas of the South, such as western and Northern Virginia and central Tennessee, where both armies regularly met in battle. Many of the inhabitants of these combat arenas fled early in the war, leaving their homes and possessions unguarded. In the later years of the war, many Northern troops marching into these regions for the first time were shocked by the desolation they encountered. In large part the destruction was due to looting, for during the first years of the conflict, both Confederate and Federal troops took whatever property struck their fancy—books, clothes, heirlooms, and so on. What they did not take, such as

[The Virginians] say they don't fear the cavalry. . . . I can only say if they don't fear the cavalry, I don't want to see those they do fear, as I see only the Cavalry, and I daily see from them acts of pillage and outrage on the poor and defence-

The Cavalry Forages

In *Hardtack and Coffee, The Unwritten Story of Army Life,* former Army of the Potomac private John D. Billings explains why the cavalry excelled at foraging, the custom in all armies of taking food from civilians, generally without payment.

There was no arm of the service that presented such favorable opportunities for foraging as did the cavalry, and none, I may add, which took so great an advantage of its opportunity. In the first place, being the eyes and the ears of the army, and usually going in advance, cavalrymen skimmed the cream off the country when a general movement was making [underway]. Then when it was settled down to camp they were the outposts and never let anything in the line of poultry, bee-hives, milk-houses, and apple-jack [apple brandy], not to enumerate [mention] other delicacies which outlying farm-houses afforded, escape the most rigid inspection. Again, they were frequently engaged in raids through the country, from the nature of which they were compelled to live in large measure off Southern products, seized as they went along; but infantry and artillery must need to confine their quests for spe-

cial rations to the homesteads near the line of march. The cavalry not only could and did search these when they led the advance, but also made requisitions on all houses in sight of the thoroughfares travelled, even when they were two or three miles away, so that, in all probability, they ate a smaller quantity of government rations, man for man, than did any other branch of the land-services.

A Federal cavalry unit returns to camp after foraging. Its speed and mobility made the cavalry ideal for scavenging and looting.

less [sic] which makes my hair stand on end and causes me to loathe all war.[47]

The slow, stretched-out marches of the two armies offered regular opportunities for soldiers to slip off to loot. In general, however, most of the marching men were focused on the coming battle, for no matter how long the walk—hours, days, or weeks—at the end of it was combat.

Chapter 6

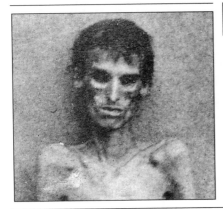

In Battle and Afterwards

Finally, it was the day of combat. The names—Bull Run, Shiloh, Antietam, Gettysburg, Chickamauga, the Wilderness, or any of a hundred lesser-known engagements of the war—changed, but constant was the drama of opposing armies massed and poised for battle.

Battle Approaches

The soldiers of both sides rose before dawn. As usual, the cavalry was up first to see to the horses. After a quick meal, each regiment formed up and then moved forward. In some cases, the troops were within a short march of the battlefield; in others, they might have long hours of marching still ahead to reach the fighting. In either case, they faced a long, grueling day, often with little or no water or food.

Approaching the battle site, soldiers and cavalry passed the field hospitals. If it was the second or third day of a battle, they saw outside the hospital tents piles of amputated arms and legs. Rows of uncovered bodies rested nearby. New soldiers, who had never been under fire, made grim jokes to hide their unease at these sights.

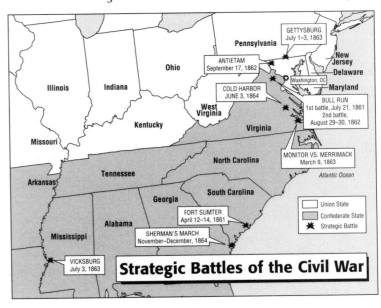

Strategic Battles of the Civil War

Veterans generally remained quiet, as they were throughout the approach.

The first troops to take the field were the artillery. Both sides engaged in what was usually an hours-long artillery duel, the purpose of which was to knock out as many of the other side's guns as possible, as well as to wipe out some of the waiting infantry and cavalry.

Final Preparations

As the cannons blasted away, each infantry and cavalry brigade prepared for battle. Infantry regiments formed two lines, one behind the other. A common formation consisted of three regiments in the front line and two in the back. Each line was itself broken into two rows of soldiers, known as ranks. Cavalry formed a single line of two ranks.

Company and squadron officers made a final inspection of weapons and ammunition. Then the colonel of each regiment or the brigade general gave a short speech or read aloud a letter from the overall army commander. Typical of the inspirational comments made at these times were those of a Union colonel who, regimental flag in hand, stepped a few feet in front of his troops and called, "Now boys is the time to write your names. Let every man do his duty. Follow me!"[48]

In some cases, these speeches were interrupted by the grim realities of war. General Thomas Meager, commander of the Union's Irish Brigade, made the rounds of his regiments at Fredericksburg, but even before he reached the last of his units, the mangled bodies of the victims of Confederate artillery were being carried from the ranks.

The Infantry Advances

The infantry brigade commander then gave the order to advance, and though a few soldiers froze, refusing to go any farther, most of the men stepped forward, rifles ready and lines straight. Across the field, their opponents stood firm, two lines ready to charge forward when necessary.

Out in front of the attacking brigade's first wave was a thin line of skirmishers. Their duty was to test the opposition's strength and to push back enemy pickets, soldiers posted out in front of the main body of troops.

The advancing infantry began to suffer losses as light artillery shells peppered its lines. When the attackers reached a point about four hundred yards from the defenders, the artillery fire changed to canister, cans filled with musket balls. Huge holes were torn in the line as men went down shredded by the deadly shot. Soldiers to the left and right of these holes closed rank so that the line remained unbroken.

At two hundred yards, rifles began to blaze. After firing, the first wave of attackers dropped to the ground and reloaded as the second wave pressed the attack. As the attacking infantry closed with the defenders, its lines broke up as soldiers surged forward. With no time to reload now, fighting became hand to hand. Screaming and cursing men battered each other, using their rifles as clubs; they kicked, and they gouged. In the end, either the attackers pushed the defenders back or were forced to retreat. The day would see a series of mass charges, until one side or the other conceded victory or withdrew.

Later in the war, as the effectiveness of artillery fire and rifles like the Springfield against massed, openly advancing troops proved devastating, some infantry units modified their tactics. They moved forward in small groups, thus presenting smaller targets that were more difficult to hit, and soldiers sought cover whenever possible. However, in general, infantry attacks remained lines of exposed men shooting at lines of equally exposed defenders.

Union troops charge Confederate forces at the Battle of Antietam. Mass attacks like this made troops vulnerable to artillery and rifle fire.

Under Fire

In the following narrative, reprinted in *The Blue and the Gray,* edited by Henry Steele Commager, Union soldier Frank Holsinger describes the battlefield as a place of both terror and joy for combatants.

At Antietam, . . . the Sixth Georgia Regiment . . . [allowed] our regiment to approach within thirty feet, and then . . . [poured] in a volley that decimated [killed or wounded] our ranks fully one-half. . . . I was stampeded. . . . I met a . . . young soldier, . . . cool as a cucumber, . . . who yelled: 'Rally, boys, rally!' . . . Instantly all fear vanished. . . . I commenced loading and firing. . . .

How natural it is for a man to suppose that if a gun is discharged, he or someone is sure to be hit. He soon finds . . . that the only damage done in ninety-nine cases out of a hundred, the only thing killed is the powder! It is not infrequently that a whole line of battle . . . will fire upon an advancing line, and no perceptible [visible] damage ensue. . . .

My sensations at Antietam were a contradiction. When . . . we were . . . passing to the front . . . the shock to the nerves was indefinable. . . . One man steps from the ranks and cowers behind a large tree, his nerves gone; he could go no farther. . . .

The battle when it goes your way is a different proposition. . . . They [the Confederates] soon begin to retire, falling back. . . . We now rush forward. We cheer, we are in ecstasies [bliss]. While shells and canister [cans filled with musket balls] are still resonant [ringing] and minies [bullets] sizzling spitefully, yet I think this one of the supreme moments of my existence.

The Cavalry Attacks

Traditionally, mounted attacks called for cavalry charges, a wave of horse soldiers riding down on the enemy. However, such mounted attacks were rare during the Civil War because charging an infantry or artillery position was suicidal. As Philip Katcher observes:

A cavalry unit 1,500 yards from a typical mid-war infantry company with 40 firing muskets . . . would take three minutes and 24 seconds to reach the men, using the typical combination of walk, trot, and final gallop. The final gallop would start at a point 400 yards from the defenders. During that time infantry could fire a total of 644 rounds of bone-breaking conical bullets into the charging mass. A charged artillery battery could get off seven rounds, ending with double canister.[49]

The few successful cavalry attacks on infantry and artillery worked because the defenders panicked and allowed themselves to be overrun or because the troops were surprised from the rear.

Cavalry charges against enemy cavalry units were more common; normally, the enemy unit responded by launching its own charge. The two forces would meet in a crash of horses. Sabers, which were of little value against infantrymen with rifles,

Cavalry Meets Cavalry

On the third day of the Battle of Gettysburg, Jeb Stuart and the Confederate cavalry attempted unsuccessfully to attack the Federal infantry from the rear. They were stopped by a far smaller Union force, which numbered George Armstrong Custer in its ranks. The bloody and violent climax of this cavalry clash, as described by Captain William C. Miller of the 3rd Pennsylvania Cavalry, is excerpted in Stephen Z. Starr's *The Union Cavalry in the Civil War.*

There appeared moving toward us a large mass of cavalry, which proved to be the re-

maining portions of [Wade] Hampton's and Fitzhugh Lee's brigades . . . formed in columns of squadrons. . . . A grander spectacle than their advance has rarely been beheld. They marched with well-aligned fronts and steady reins. Their polished saber-blades dazzled in the sun. . . . Shell and shrapnel met the advancing Confederates and tore through their ranks. Closing their ranks as though nothing had happened, on they came. As they came nearer, canister [cans filled with musket balls] was substituted . . . for shell, and horse after horse staggered and fell. Still they came on. . . . The 1st Michigan, drawn up in close column of squadrons . . . , was ordered . . . to charge. Custer . . . placed himself at its head, and off they dashed. As the two columns approached each other, the pace of each increased. . . . So sudden and violent was the collision [of Northern and Southern cavalry] that many of the horses were turned end over end and crushed their riders beneath them. The clashing of sabers, the firing of pistols, the demands for surrender, and cries of the combatants, filled the air.

George Armstrong Custer leads the 1st Michigan against Jeb Stuart's cavalry unit, halting the Confederates' advance.

proved effective against other saber-wielding soldiers. However, some cavalry commanders preferred revolvers or carbines to swords, and the Confederate general Nathan Bedford Forrest armed his troopers with shotguns.

On the battlefield, cavalry were most useful as a quick-strike mounted infantry. The horse soldiers would ride quickly to a place where the battle was going poorly for their side; dismount, leaving one man in four to hold the horses; and move in, firing their carbines. Since many Federal cavalry units used repeating rifles during the last half of the war, a small band of cavalrymen could take on a much larger infantry force. On the first day at Gettysburg, for instance, two brigades of Union horse soldiers held off a Confederate division twice their strength until Union infantry reinforcements came up.

Rebel Yells and Battle Deafness

Whether on foot or on horseback, the fighting men yelled or cheered as they attacked and counterattacked. Northerners gave forth with a sustained hurrah. Southerners filled the air with the famous Rebel yell, which one Federal soldier described as "a succession of canine yelps, which at a distance from its shrillness seemed like the sound of boys' voices, but when near was terror striking from its savagery."[50] This yell, rendered in slightly different ways in different parts of the South, frightened Union troops, particularly men new to combat. Like the Union hurrah, it was an intense release of pent-up fright and excitement.

But at times even the high-pitched Rebel yell could not pierce the deafening din of battle. Human voices were raised as officers and sergeants shouted orders, and the wounded shrieked and screamed in pain. Cannons roared, rifles and revolvers crackled, drums were beaten, and trumpets sounded. One Confederate soldier said that he could not hear his own rifle, the sounds of battle were so loud.

Gun Smoke and Confusion

As the day wore on, soldiers and cavalry, friend and foe, were engulfed in smoke: Smokeless gunpowder was not developed until after the Civil War. Consequently, often soldiers and cavalry troopers could locate specific units only by the battle flags that waved above the drifting clouds of gun smoke.

The smoke added to the general confusion of battle. No one could be sure what was going on or who was winning. In parts of the field, entire commands became so intermixed that the officers no longer knew whose men were whose. In other places, the fighting became a struggle between small groups of combatants, acting independently because they had long since been cut off from their commanders.

The Price of Battle

After hour upon hour of fighting, even fit soldiers were close to physical collapse. Wiley writes that

> Though accustomed before the war to long hours of labor on the farm . . . , [the Civil War soldier] found fighting the hardest work he had ever done. Fatigue was sharpened by the fact that rest and food had been scarce during the days before the battle. By midafternoon his strength was often so depleted [drained] that he could hardly load and fire his gun, if indeed he was able to stand at all.[51]

With night came the end of the fighting, but not necessarily the end of battle, which might continue for days. For the moment, however, the survivors took their bearings, numbed and dazed by the noise and confusion of combat, and their hands and faces smeared black with gunpowder. They stumbled back to their own lines, rejoining the companies from which they had become separated, and learned who among their messmates were missing. Too tired to cook, they ate cold rations and then tried to sleep.

In the background were the moans and screams of the wounded, many of whom would die during the night. The dead disturbed no one, at least not until daylight. Then, the true cost of the war revealed itself in heaps of bodies and body parts. Some regiments, such as the 1st Texas at Antietam or the 1st Minnesota at Gettysburg, sustained over 80 percent casualties.

Being Wounded

Being wounded in the Civil War was a fearsome business. Even getting from the battlefield to the hospital was hazardous. It was not until the middle of the war that either side created a corps of medics whose only job was to cart the wounded to field hospitals. Before then, the wounded might be picked up by members of the regimental band, or they might not be picked up at all. In the latter case, a wounded man might lie for hours, sometimes even a day, before help arrived.

Dead soldiers lie on the field after the Battle of Gettysburg. Some regiments suffered over 80 percent casualties during the fight.

Those who made it to the field hospital were not necessarily better off. Medical knowledge was still primitive and doctors had few effective ways of treating injured soldiers. They had chloroform and ether to knock out their patients during surgery. They had opium to control pain. However, they had no antibiotics or sterilization procedures to prevent infection, which killed thousands of soldiers.

Additionally, military doctors of the period were often poorly trained; many joined the service only because they had failed in civilian practice. Many were drunk much of the time. Not surprisingly, soldiers on both sides were afraid to be treated. One Alabama soldier said, "I believes [sic] the doctors kill more than they cure," and an Illinois private observed, "Our doctor knows about as much as a ten-year-old boy."[52]

Battlefield Surgery

Soldiers shot in the gut generally died. Those wounded in an extremity were luckier: Though bullets often shattered the bones of arms and legs, forcing routine removal of the limb, the overall chance of survival was greater.

A wounded man slated for amputation was placed on a table covered with a rubber sheet. If chloroform or ether was available, the soldier was knocked out. Even without anesthesia, the limb still came off: The wounded man, often screaming and thrashing, had to be held down by surgical assistants.

Treating the Wounded

After the Battle of Gettysburg, Carl Schurz, commander of the Army of the Potomac's XI Corps, visited the hospital area. He left the following report of his observations which can be found in *The Blue and the Gray*, edited by Henry Steele Commager.

> To look after the wounded of my command, I visited the places where the surgeons were at work. . . . At Gettysburg the wounded—many thousands of them— were carried to the farmsteads behind our lines. The houses, barns, the sheds, the open barnyards were crowded with moaning and wailing human beings. . . . A heavy rain set in . . . and large numbers had to remain unprotected in the open. I saw long rows of men lying under the eaves of the buildings, the water pouring down upon their bodies in streams. . . .
>
> There stood the surgeons, their sleeves rolled up to the elbows, their bare arms as well as their linen aprons smeared with blood, their knives . . . held between their teeth, while they were helping a patient on or off the table . . . ; around them pools of blood and amputated arms or legs in heaps, sometimes more than man-high. . . . As a wounded man was lifted on the table, often shrieking with pain as the attendants handled him, the surgeon quickly examined the wound and resolved upon cutting off the injured limb. Some ether was administered. . . . The surgeon snatched his knife from between his teeth . . . , wiped it rapidly once or twice across his blood-stained apron, and the cutting began.

The spread of infection by germs was as yet undiscovered, so nothing was kept clean. Between operations, the rubber sheet might or might not be sponged off. Surgeons would rinse instruments in a pan of bloody water and then wipe them dry with a dirty rag.

Nurses in the Civil War

Many nurses in Civil War hospitals, particularly field hospitals, were men. Notable among this group was nineteenth-century American poet Walt Whitman.

Women in both the North and the South also nursed the thousands of sick and wounded soldiers. By the war's end, some ten thousand women had volunteered as nurses.

Many Northern and Southern doctors did not trust women as nurses and limited their duties to housecleaning and laundry details. However, other doctors came to see the value of these women volunteers, and the duties of women nurses expanded. As one Southern nurse described, they "[sat] up all night, bathing the men's wounds, and giving them water."[53] They gave medicine, they bandaged wounds, they assisted in surgery, and they supervised other nurses.

In June 1861, the U.S. Army asked Dorothea Lynde Dix to oversee Union female nurses. Dix, a campaigner for medical reform, particularly for the mentally ill, required among other things that each nurse be approved by two doctors, be at least thirty years old, and be able to cook. For uniforms, most Union nurses simply wore dark civilian clothes.

In the South, no corps of women nurses existed for the first year and a half of the war. But in all regions of the Confederacy, hundreds of women volunteered to nurse soldiers. These women had to overcome the Southern prejudice that a military hospital was no place for a lady. In September 1862, the Confederate Congress, realizing the importance of women nurses, passed a law calling for women to work in military hospitals.

Clara Barton

Clara Barton, known as "the Angel of the Battlefield," was one of the most famous nurses of the Civil War. Born in 1821 in Oxford, Massachusetts, she was a former schoolteacher working as a clerk in the Patent Office when war broke out.

Barton first treated wounded soldiers in 1861 when Federal troops who had been attacked by Southern sympathizers in Baltimore were brought to Washington, D.C. Unaffiliated with any Federal or civilian relief agency, she operated on her own.

When not organizing large-scale relief efforts, Barton personally took medicines and supplies to front-line soldiers, thus earning her nickname. In September 1862, she followed the Army of the Potomac's II Corps into battle at Antietam, driving a wagon onto the battlefield. There she helped doctors treat the wounded, at one point even removing a bullet from the cheek of one soldier and assisting a Union doctor at the moment he was shot dead.

Near the end of the war, Lincoln asked Barton to compile a list of missing and dead soldiers. This job took her to the no-

Clara Barton, "the Angel of the Battlefield," was one of the most well known nurses of the Civil War.

the beginning of the war, both sides had agreed to exchange prisoners. Privates were exchanged one for one; depending upon their rank, officers were rated in value to a specified number of private soldiers.

The exchange system, however, broke down, beginning in 1863 when the two sides could not agree on whether civilians captured in the border states of Missouri, Kentucky, or Maryland would or should be exchanged. An additional snag was the Confederacy's refusal to recognize captured black troops as prisoners of war. Finally, when Ulysses S. Grant took over Union forces, he saw that the North held more Confederates than the South did Federals. He did not want to return soldiers to the man-hungry Southern armies, and the North, with its larger population, could make do without those Union prisoners.

Prison Camps

Most prisons were converted camps of instruction, whose barracks housed captured men; converted structures, such as the tobacco warehouse that became Libby Prison in Richmond; tented compounds; or bare stockades, where shelter was left to the prisoners' devices.

The Confederacy's Andersonville in Georgia was the largest and most notorious of all Civil War prisons. Set up in early 1864, this stockade camp was meant to hold 10,000 prisoners. The population soon exceeded this capacity, and by the summer of 1864 topped 32,000. In its fifteen months of operation, 50,000 prisoners

torious Confederate prison of Andersonville, where she recorded the names of thousands of Union prisoners of war who had died there.

Prisoners of War

The Andersonville prison camp was one of the approximately 150 military prisons established by both sides to hold captured soldiers. Union and Confederate forces captured hundreds of thousands of enemy troops during the four years of fighting. At were put into the Georgia prison. A quarter of these men, some 12,000, died of starvation and disease. After the war was over, the camp's commanding officer, Captain Henry Wirz, was tried and executed for war crimes.

As bad as Andersonville was, no prison camp on either side was good. Like the Georgia camp, they were all filthy, disease-ridden, and overcrowded. Inmates were routinely underfed and underclothed. And the overall death rate was roughly the same for the North and South; 26,000 died in Northern camps, 22,000 in Southern camps. Indeed, New York's Elmira Prison, although considerably smaller than Ander-

Andersonville

The Confederacy's Andersonville was the most notorious of a bad lot of military prisons on both sides of the Civil War. Eliza Andrews, a Georgia woman, left an account of conditions within the prison as told to her by Catholic priest Father Hamilton, reprinted in *The Blue and the Gray*, edited by Henry Steele Commager.

Although matters have improved somewhat with the cool weather [of January 1865], the tales that are told of the condition of things there last summer are appalling. . . . Father Hamilton [said] . . . that during the summer the wretched prisoners burrowed in the ground like moles to protect themselves from the sun. It was not safe to give them material to build shanties as they might use it for clubs to overpower the guard. These underground huts . . . were alive with vermin and stank like charnel houses. Many of the prisoners were stark naked, having not so much a shirt to their backs. . . .

Father Hamilton said that at one time the prisoners died at the rate of a hundred and fifty a day, and he saw some of them die on the ground without a rag to lie on or a garment to cover them. Dysentery was the most fatal disease, and as they lay on the ground in their own excrements, the smell was so horrible that the good father says that he was often obliged to rush from their presence to get a breath of pure air. . . . I am afraid that God will suffer some terrible retribution [punishment] to fall upon us for letting such things happen.

This skeletal Union soldier was a survivor of Andersonville.

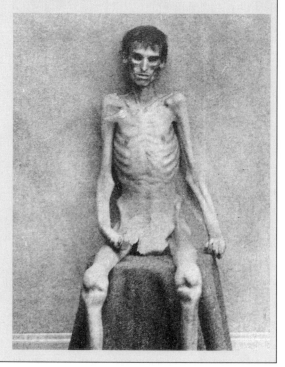

sonville, also killed a quarter of its prison population, some 3,000 of 12,000 inmates.

Wirz thus was no more or less guilty than any other prison commandant on either side. The real culprit was the war itself. Both North and South were fighting an all-out battle and had nothing to spare for the military prisons, which were last in line to receive food, clothing, and medicine.

A wounded Confederate soldier is nursed back to health by a Yankee family. Such acts of kindness were common on both sides during the Civil War.

Gallantry in Action

Amid the horrors of the battlefield, the hospital, and the prison, were acts of surprising kindness and generosity, for the Civil War was a strange combination of the brutal and the gallant. During the most terrible slaughter, men of both sides would offer aid to their wounded or dying enemies. Wounded Union private Rice C. Bull and other injured Federals were picked up by Confederates during the Battle of Chancellorsville. Bull later wrote that "all the Johnnies treated us with kindness. . . . Without exception [I] found them kind and helpful."[54]

Later, at Gettysburg, Confederate general John B. Gordon spied a Union officer who, in Gordon's words,

> went down pierced by a [bullet]. . . . Quickly dismounting and lifting his head, I gave him water from my canteen, asked his name. . . . He was . . .

General Francis C. Barlow of New York. . . . The [bullet] had entered his body in front and passed out near the spinal cord, paralyzing him in legs and arms. Neither of us had the remotest thought that he could possibly survive for many hours. I summoned several soldiers . . . [to] carry him to the shade in the rear.[55]

Barlow not only lived but regained the use of his arms and legs. Years later, the two men met again and became lifelong friends. Indeed, when the war ended and the men in blue and gray went home, they would find that it was their former comrades and enemies with whom they now had most in common.

Returning Home

Late May 1865; the war was over. The Union victory was complete. The Confederate armies had surrendered, and the Confederacy was no more. Although the South would be occupied by Federal troops for the next decade, the period of Reconstruction, the victors would take little vengeance. Few former Confederates served jail terms and even fewer were executed. Confederate president Jefferson Davis would spend two years imprisoned at Fort Monroe, Virginia, and then be released without ever coming to trial. Confederate military leaders such as Robert E. Lee were allowed to return to civilian life in whatever capacity they wished.

For the soldiers and cavalry of the two armies, it was time to go home. Many in the North found it relatively easy to pick up their old lives. The lot of defeated Southerners returning to a war-damaged land was harder. However, many Federal as well as

Confederate president Jefferson Davis (left) spent two years in prison after the war. General Robert E. Lee (right) was allowed to return to civilian life.

Confederate veterans would eventually find that their four years of combat set them apart from those who remained at home.

The Grand Review

The final act of the war for many of the Union soldiers and cavalry was the Grand Review, a parade of army troops. At the suggestion of Secretary of War Edwin Stanton, the Federal Armies of the Potomac, Tennessee, and Georgia, over a quarter-million men, paraded through the streets of Washington in a huge victory celebration. So many soldiers participated that the event took two days, May 23 and 24.

The city was decorated, triumphal arches erected, and viewing stands placed everywhere. Those without seats stood lining the streets; many participants from the first day joined the crowds of spectators on the second. Delegations from every state in the Union cheered their loudest when their state regiments marched past. Rice Bull wrote that

> We . . . were given great applause by the hundreds of thousands of spectators who lined the streets of Washington for miles. . . . There were thousands of soldiers . . . who had marched the day before. . . ; they shouted themselves

Victorious Union soldiers parade through Washington, D.C., during the Grand Review of May 23–24, 1865.

hoarse. . . . It was a proud day for all of us, and the Review was a fitting ending of our long service.[56]

Final Muster

After the Grand Review, most of the troops boarded boats or trains for the trip back to their home states, where they made one final camp. There they turned in equipment and weapons, although they were allowed to buy their rifles and carbines if they so desired. Their discharge papers and final pay were issued, along with any bounty money due. The average soldier received $250, a great deal of money in mid-nineteenth-century America. Some had to pay for lost equipment out of this sum, some lost it to gamblers and thieves, but most took it home to invest in businesses and farms.

After being paid and receiving their discharge papers, the soldiers and cavalry troopers assembled for a last regimental review. Regimental and company officers each said a few words, then dismissed the men. The former soldiers shook hands and left to make their way home, singly or in small groups.

Once home, they did their best to reenter the civilian world. One Union lieutenant arrived to find his father cutting corn: "I doffed [took off] my uniform . . . , put on some . . . old clothes, armed myself with a corn knife, and proceeded to wage war on the standing corn . . . as if I had been away only a day or two."[57]

In the South

For the Confederates, everything was different. There was no parade, no final muster, no pay, and no transportation home. After relinquishing their weapons to Federal troops, Southern soldiers might or might not have a few last words from their commanding officer. Then they were on their own, generally penniless since many had not been paid in a year and others held only worthless Confederate scrip.

The South's railway system had been destroyed in the war, so most of the former Confederates had to walk home. Some cavalry troopers were able to keep their horses, but even so it was often a long way back, particularly if they had been serving in Virginia and their homes were in Mississippi or even Texas.

The scattering soldiers had very little food and, lacking money, were reduced to begging or stealing. They soon found that many Southern civilians resented them, thinking them cowards for having lost the war. The former soldiers' constant scrounging for food also drew civilian contempt. The soldiers found few among the Southern population who understood what they had been through.

On reaching home, the men found further problems. Katcher writes:

> When they finally got home, they often found their property in ruins, the fields untended, fence and buildings down and taxes not paid. Small things that had worn out or been broken or lost, things like pins and pocket knives, were impossible to replace. [58]

Post-Traumatic Stress Syndrome

Civilians of the North were much more friendly toward their returning troops, for these men had won the war. Yet, like their Southern counterparts, Northern veterans soon discovered that fellow citizens who had not gone to war did not understand the former soldiers' experiences on and off the battlefield.

Many veterans, North and South, found themselves depressed for years after the war, suffering from what is now called post-traumatic stress syndrome, a condi-

Many Confederate soldiers returned home only to find their houses destroyed and their property in ruins.

tion describing, in the aftermath of some terrible episode, depression, withdrawal, anger, and occasionally violent behavior. The most severely affected Civil War veterans could not readjust to civilian life; some lost job after job, some migrated west or lived alone in the woods; some began drinking; some even killed themselves.

The Grand Army of the Republic

By no means did all former Confederates and Federals suffer from post-traumatic stress syndrome, and many who did were able to work through it as the years passed and as memories of the war dimmed.

Indeed, any number began to miss the excitement of the war and, more importantly, the close companionship of their fellow soldiers. In a desire to rekindle this

bond, as early as 1866, veterans in the North formed the Grand Army of the Republic (GAR). Some units even formed their own veterans groups, such as the 57th Massachusetts Infantry Regimental Association.

At its height in 1890, the GAR claimed a half-million members. The organization had posts, or local clubs in every major Northern city. Its aims were "fraternity, commemoration, and assistance to its members. It was active in establishing [old] soldiers' homes . . . and in caring for and educating soldiers' orphans."[59]

Although the GAR was neutral politically, its members—and indeed all former Civil War servicemen—were a major political force. Between the war's end in 1865 and 1900, seven of the eight presidents of the United States had served in the Union army.

The United Confederate Veterans

Confederate veterans organized much later than their fellows in the North. They were the losers of the war, and many preferred not to look back. Yet, by 1889 numbers of former Southern soldiers found that, like Northern veterans, they missed and desired to reestablish old wartime friendships, so they formed the United Confederate Veterans (UCV).

Before long the GAR and the UCV began to hold joint celebrations, called

Former enemies shake hands at a reunion held during the fiftieth anniversary of the Battle of Gettysburg.

In 1913 the two veteran groups joined in a show of unity. Fifty-four thousand Federal and Confederate veterans met in July of that year at Gettysburg to commemorate the fiftieth anniversary of the battle.

On July 3, 180 Federal veterans climbed atop and stood in formation along Cemetery Ridge in the position they had defended fifty years before. Facing them on the flat farmland below, a line of 120 Confederate survivors of the disastrous Pickett's charge marched quietly forward. When they reached the Northern veterans, the Southerners reached out and shook hands with their former foes. Onlookers cheered.

This sense of unity between onetime enemies was expressed in the 1920s by John Mason, a veteran of the Confederate artillery. "I fired a cannon," Mason said when questioned about his war activities. "I hope I never kill[ed] any one."[60]

encampments. The two groups, despite being on different sides in the Civil War, had experienced and suffered much in common. In fundamental ways, they understood each other.

⋆ Notes ⋆

Introduction: War Between the States

1. Samuel Carter III, *The Last Cavaliers: Confederate and Union Cavalry in the Civil War.* New York: St. Martin's, 1979, p. 3.
2. Quoted in James M. McPherson, *Battle Cry of Freedom: The Civil War Era.* Oxford: Oxford University Press, 1988, p. 337.
3. Quoted in James M. McPherson, ed., *The Atlas of the Civil War.* New York: Macmillan, 1994, p. 95.
4. Quoted in Henry Steele Commager, ed., *The Blue and the Gray: Two Volumes in One: The Story of the Civil War as Told by Participants.* New York: Fairfax Press, 1960, p. 643.

Chapter 1: Joining Up

5. Quoted in James I. Robertson Jr., *Soldiers Blue and Gray.* Columbia: University of South Carolina Press, 1988, pp. 13–14.
6. Bell Irvin Wiley, *The Life of Billy Yank: The Common Soldier of the Union.* Indianapolis: Bobbs-Merrill, 1952, pp. 32–33.
7. Carter, *The Last Cavaliers*, p. 6.
8. Quoted in Bell Irvin Wiley, *They Who Fought Here.* New York: Macmillan, 1959, p. 26.
9. Quoted in Philip Katcher, *The Civil War Source Book.* New York: Facts On File, 1992, p. 97.
10. Robertson, *Soldiers Blue and Gray*, p. 3.
11. Wiley, *They Who Fought Here*, p. 5.
12. Stephen Z. Starr, *The Union Cavalry in the Civil War,* vol. 1. Baton Rouge: Louisiana State University Press, 1979, pp. 109–10.
13. Quoted in Carter, *The Last Cavaliers*, p. 7.

Chapter 2: Uniforms and Rifles

14. Quoted in Katcher, *The Civil War Source Book*, p. 213.
15. Carter, *The Last Cavaliers*, p. 6.
16. Quoted in Jack Coggins, *Arms and Equipment of the Civil War.* New York: Fairfax Press, 1962, p. 29.
17. Wiley, *They Who Fought Here*, p. 121.
18. Quoted in Bell Irvin Wiley, *The Life of Johnny Reb: The Common Soldier of the Confederacy.* Indianapolis: Bobbs-Merrill, 1943, p. 307.
19. Quoted in Wiley, *The Life of Johnny Reb*, p. 307.
20. Starr, *The Union Cavalry in the Civil War,* vol. 1, p. 130.
21. Quoted in Starr, *The Union Cavalry in the Civil War,* vol. 1, p. 131.
22. Quoted in Wiley, *They Who Fought Here*, p. 77.

Chapter 3: Training and Discipline

23. William J. Miller, *The Training of an Army: Camp Curtin and the North's Civil War.* Shippensburg, PA: White Mane, 1990, p. v.
24. Quoted in Robertson, *Soldiers Blue and Gray*, p. 51.
25. Quoted in Robertson, *Soldiers Blue and Gray*, p. 49.
26. Quoted in Wiley, *They Who Fought Here*, p. 42.
27. Quoted in Starr, *The Union Cavalry in the Civil War*, vol. 1, p. 139.
28. Quoted in Robertson, *Soldiers Blue and Gray*, p. 123.
29. Coggins, *Arms and Equipment of the Civil War*, p. 10.
30. Quoted in Commager, *The Blue and the Gray*, pp. 509–13.

Chapter 4: In Camp

31. Quoted in Wiley, *They Who Fought Here*, p. 38.
32. John D. Billings, *Hardtack and Coffee: The Unwritten Story of Army Life.* Bowie, MD: Heritage Books, 1887, p. 196.
33. Starr, *The Union Cavalry in the Civil War*, vol. 1, p. 24.
34. Quoted in Robertson, *Soldiers Blue and Gray*, p. 44.
35. Quoted in Robertson, *Soldiers Blue and Gray*, pp. 46–47.
36. Quoted in Robertson, *Soldiers Blue and Gray*, p. 65.
37. Quoted in Starr, *The Union Cavalry in the Civil War*, vol. 1, p. 194.
38. Quoted in Wiley, *They Who Fought Here*, p. 145.
39. Robertson, *Soldiers Blue and Gray*, p. 140.

Chapter 5: On the March

40. Wiley, *They Who Fought Here*, p. 243.
41. Quoted in Starr, *The Union Cavalry in the Civil War*, vol. 1, p. 110.
42. Frank Wilkeson, *Turned Inside Out: Recollections of a Private Soldier in the Army of the Potomac.* Lincoln: University of Nebraska Press, 1886, p. 41.
43. Robertson, *Soldiers Blue and Gray*, p. 60.
44. Rice C. Bull, *Soldiering: The Civil War Diary of Rice C. Bull, 123rd New York Volunteer Infantry.* Ed. K. Jack Bauer. Novato, CA: Presidio Press, 1977, p. 29.
45. Bull, *Soldiering*, p. 21.
46. Quoted in Wiley, *The Life of Johnny Reb*, p. 46.
47. Quoted in Starr, *The Union Cavalry in the Civil War*, vol. 1, p. 257.

Chapter 6: In Battle and Afterwards

48. Quoted in Wiley, *The Life of Billy Yank*, p. 68.
49. Katcher, *The Civil War Source Book*, p. 79.
50. Quoted in Wiley, *They Who Fought Here*, p. 257.
51. Wiley, *The Life of Johnny Reb*, p. 73.
52. Quoted in McPherson, *Battle Cry of Freedom*, p. 486.
53. Quoted in McPherson, *Battle Cry of Freedom*, p. 479.
54. Bull, *Soldiering*, p. 63.
55. Quoted in Richard Wheeler, ed., *Voices of the Civil War.* New York: Crowell, 1976, pp. 295–96.

Conclusion: Returning Home

56. Bull, *Soldiering,* p. 248.

57. Quoted in Katcher, *The Civil War Source Book,* p. 128.

58. Katcher, *The Civil War Source Book,* p. 128.

59. Francis A. Lord, *They Fought for the Union.* Harrisburg, PA: Stackpole, 1960, pp. 332–33.

60. Quoted in Robertson, *Soldiers Blue and Gray,* p. 227.

☆ Chronology of Events ☆

1860

November 6: Abraham Lincoln is elected president of the United States.

December 20: South Carolina becomes the first state to secede from the Union.

1861

January: A second Southern state, Mississippi, secedes, followed by Florida, Alabama, Georgia, and Louisiana.

February 1: Texas secedes.

February 10: Jefferson Davis is elected president of the Confederate States of America.

March 4: Lincoln is inaugurated.

April 12: War breaks out when Confederate forces fire on Fort Sumter in the harbor of Charleston, South Carolina.

April 17–18: Virginia secedes; Robert E. Lee resigns his commission in the United States Army.

April 19: Lincoln orders a naval blockade of the Confederacy.

April 23: Lee becomes commander in chief of Virginia's armed forces.

May: Richmond, Virginia, becomes the capital of the Confederacy, and Arkansas and North Carolina join the Confederacy.

June 8: Tennessee becomes the final state to secede.

July 21: Confederate forces defeat Union troops at the First Battle of Bull Run near Manassas, Virginia, twenty-five miles south of Washington, D.C.

July 28: Lee takes command of Confederate forces in western Virginia.

November 1: Lincoln appoints George B. McClellan commander in chief of the United States Army; McClellan begins assembling the Army of the Potomac.

November 8: A Union warship intercepts the British steamer *Trent* and arrests two Confederate diplomats, an act that outrages the British government.

1862

February 25: Union troops capture Nashville, Tennessee.

March 4: Lee becomes military adviser to Jefferson Davis.

March 9: The Union ironclad *Monitor* defeats the Confederate ironclad *Virginia* (formerly the Union warship *Merrimac*) at Hampton Roads, Virginia.

March 11: Lincoln removes McClellan as commander in chief but leaves him in command of the Army of the Potomac.

April 4: McClellan and the Army of the Potomac begin the Peninsular Campaign, an attempt to capture Richmond.

April 6–7: Union forces commanded by

Ulysses S. Grant win the Battle of Shiloh in Tennessee.

April 25: Union naval forces under the command of David Farragut capture New Orleans.

June 1: Davis appoints Lee commander of Confederate forces at Richmond; Lee names his new command the Army of Northern Virginia.

June 6: Union forces capture Memphis, Tennessee.

June 25–July 1: The Peninsular Campaign ends when the Army of Northern Virginia drives the Army of the Potomac away from Richmond in the Seven Days' Battle.

August 29–30: The Army of Northern Virginia defeats the Army of the Potomac at the Second Battle of Bull Run at Manassas, Virginia.

September 4: Lee and the Army of Northern Virginia cross the Potomac River into Maryland in their first invasion of the Union.

September 17: The Army of the Potomac defeats the Army of Northern Virginia at the Battle of Antietam near Sharpsburg, Maryland; the Confederates retreat to Virginia.

September 22: Lincoln issues the Emancipation Proclamation, which frees all slaves in the Confederate states.

November 3: Union forces under Grant begin the first campaign to capture Vicksburg, Mississippi.

November 7: Lincoln appoints Ambrose E. Burnside to replace McClellan as com-

mander of the Army of the Potomac.

December 13: The Army of Northern Virginia defeats the Army of the Potomac at the Battle of Fredericksburg in Virginia.

December 29: A Confederate victory at Chickasaw Bluffs, Mississippi, over Union troops led by William T. Sherman ends the Union's first Vicksburg Campaign.

1863

January 8: Grant launches the second Vicksburg Campaign.

January 26: Joseph Hooker replaces Burnside as commander of the Army of the Potomac.

March 3: Lincoln signs the Federal Draft Act.

May 1–4: The Army of Northern Virginia defeats the Army of the Potomac at the Battle of Chancellorsville in Virginia; Confederate general Thomas "Stonewall" Jackson is mortally wounded.

May 18: Union forces under Grant besiege Vicksburg.

June 3: The Army of Northern Virginia begins its march north in its second invasion of the Union.

June 9: Confederate cavalry units commanded by General Jeb Stuart drive off Union cavalry at Brandy Station, Virginia.

June 15: The Army of Northern Virginia crosses the Potomac River into Maryland.

June 24: Advance units of the Army of Northern Virginia reach Pennsylvania.

June 28: General George Meade replaces Hooker as commander of the Army of the Potomac.

July 1–3: The Army of the Potomac defeats the Army of Northern Virginia at the Battle of Gettysburg in Pennsylvania.

July 4: The Army of Northern Virginia retreats to Virginia; Grant's troops take Vicksburg, giving complete control of the Mississippi River to the Union, thus cutting the Confederacy in two.

July 13–16: Draft riots erupt in New York City.

September 19–20: Confederate forces defeat Union troops at the Battle of Chickamauga in Tennessee.

November 19: Lincoln delivers the Gettysburg Address.

November 23–25: Union forces win the Battle of Chattanooga in Tennessee.

1864

March 9: Lincoln makes Grant general in chief of the United States Army.

May 5–7: Grant and the Army of the Potomac engage Lee and the Army of Northern Virginia at the Battle of the Wilderness in Virginia; although the Confederates claim victory, Grant advances toward Richmond.

May 7: Sherman begins his campaign to capture Atlanta, Georgia.

May 11: Confederate calvary leader Jeb Stuart is mortally wounded.

June 16–18: The Army of the Potomac besieges Petersburg, Virginia, only twenty miles south of Richmond.

August 5: Farragut leads a fleet that captures Mobile Bay, Alabama.

September 2: Sherman's troops capture Atlanta.

November 8: Lincoln is elected to a second term as president.

November 15: Leaving much of Atlanta in ruins, Sherman begins his march across Georgia to the sea.

December 21: Sherman captures Savannah, Georgia.

1865

February 1: Sherman turns his forces north against South Carolina.

March 29: Grant launches his final campaign against the Army of Northern Virginia.

March 30–April 1: The Army of the Potomac defeats the Army of Northern Virginia at the Battle of Five Forks in Virginia.

April 2: Union forces take Petersburg and then Richmond; as the Confederate capital burns, Lee and the Army of Northern Virginia retreat, while Davis and the Confederate government flee.

April 9: Lee surrenders to Grant at Appomattox Court House, Virginia.

April 14: John Wilkes Booth mortally wounds Lincoln at Ford's Theater; Union troops hold victory celebration at Fort Sumter.

April 26: Confederate general Joseph E. Johnston surrenders to Sherman.

May 10: Union cavalry captures Jefferson Davis in Georgia.

May 13: Confederate forces defeat Union troops at Palmito Ranch, Texas, in the final battle of the Civil War.

May 26: Union general Edward Canby accepts the surrender of the last active Confederate troops.

⋆ **For Further Reading** ⋆

Timothy L. Biel, *Life in the North During the Civil War.* San Diego: Lucent Books, 1997. Filled with photographs and eyewitness accounts, this study examines the effects of the war on the North and the diverse reactions and opinions of Northerners to the conflict.

James A. Corrick, *The Battle of Gettysburg.* San Diego: Lucent Books, 1996. Supported by reports of participants, maps, and period photographs, this detailed account describes the events that led up to this conflict, the battle itself, and the aftermath. Additional material includes a time line and a reading list.

Stephen Crane, *The Red Badge of Courage.* New York: Bantam Classics, 1981. This classic novel presents a graphic and realistic picture of the Civil War battlefield. In clear, vivid prose, the author brings to life a young recruit's first day in combat.

Stephen Currie, *Slavery.* San Diego: Greenhaven Press, 1998. Airs the pros and cons of the nineteenth-century debate on slavery, letting those involved speak for themselves. Includes a bibliography, statistics, and a list of important documents.

William Dudley, ed., *The Civil War.* San Diego: Greenhaven Press, 1994. A collection of period writings that present in chronological order and in pro/con format the issues that led up to the war and that led to internal divisions within North and South during the conflict.

Hamlin Garland, "The Return of a Private," in *Main-Traveled Roads.* New York: New American Library, 1891. A classic short story that effectively details the homecoming of one midwestern Union soldier.

David Haugen and Lori Shein, *The Civil War.* San Diego: Greenhaven Press, 1998. Presents opposing viewpoints on the important issues of the war, from slavery to secession to the role of black soldiers. Relies on generous primary and secondary source quotations and includes a bibliography and list of important documents.

Joe Kirchberger, *The Civil War and Reconstruction.* New York: Facts On File, 1991. A good, short history of the Civil War and its aftermath that is enriched by many passages taken from letters, diaries, and newspapers of the time. The text is also supported by photographs, maps, and a bibliography.

Stephen R. Lilley, *Fighters Against American Slavery.* San Diego: Lucent Books, 1999.

Through biographical sketches of important abolitionists such as William Lloyd Garrison and Frederick Douglass, and other opponents of slavery such as Nat Turner, the history of the running battle against slavery emerges. Supplemental material includes photographs, eyewitness accounts, and a reading list.

James P. Reger, *The Battle of Antietam*. San Diego: Lucent Books, 1997. Describes this campaign and the events surrounding it, as well as examining the battle's effects, particularly as they influenced Lincoln to issue the Emancipation Proclamation. Text is accompanied by photographs, quotations, a time line, and a reading list.

————, *Civil War Generals of the Confederacy*. San Diego: Lucent Books, 1999. Individual biographies of such Confederate military leaders as Robert E. Lee, Jeb Stuart, and Stonewall Jackson reveal the qualities that brought them victories against the odds. Supported by photographs, quotations, and a reading list.

————, *Life in the South During the Civil War*. San Diego: Lucent Books, 1997. Examines the way Southerners viewed the Civil War as an invasion and the Northern victory as the bitter end of their chosen way of life. The text is supported by many period photographs, quotations from the time, and a reading list.

Robert Hunt Rhodes, ed., *All for the Union*. New York: Crown, 1991. A firsthand account of the everyday life of a Union soldier as told through the letters and diary of Elisha Hunt Rhodes. Rhodes, who entered the army as a nineteen-year-old private and left it four years later as a colonel, fought in every major eastern battle from First Bull Run to Appomattox.

Annette Tapert, ed., *The Brothers' War: Civil War Letters to Their Loved Ones from the Blue and Gray*. New York: Random House, 1988. A collection of letters by both Union and Confederate soldiers that reveals how these men saw the war in which they fought. Photographs, which include some of the letter writers, illustrate the text.

Rafael Tilton, *Clara Barton*. San Diego: Lucent Books, 1995. A readable biography of the life of the famed Civil War nurse and her later role in founding the American Red Cross. Extensive quotations from the period, a time line of Barton's life, and a reading list add to the value of the text.

Geoffrey C. Ward et al., *The Civil War: An Illustrated History*. New York: Knopf, 1991. Lavishly illustrated with photographs, drawings, and maps, this companion volume to the PBS Civil War Series presents a solid, short history of the conflict.

Diane Yancey, *Civil War Generals of the Union*. San Diego: Lucent Books, 1999. Traces the lives of such Union commanders as Grant, McClellan, and Sherman, revealing the qualities that brought them success or failure. Many photographs and quotations round out the individual portraits.

★ Works Consulted ★

John D. Billings, *Hardtack and Coffee: The Unwritten Story of Army Life.* Bowie, MD: Heritage Books, 1887. This memoir of Civil War army life by a Union veteran is filled with solid information on every aspect of a soldier's life. Numerous drawings are valuable additions to the text.

Rice C. Bull, *Soldiering: The Civil War Diary of Rice C. Bull, 123rd New York Volunteer Infantry.* Ed. K. Jack Bauer. Novato, CA: Presidio Press, 1977. An informative day-to-day record of service in the Army of the Potomac from September 1862 to June 1865.

Samuel Carter III, *The Last Cavaliers: Confederate and Union Cavalry in the Civil War.* New York: St. Martin's, 1979. Traces the history of both Union and Confederate cavalry, focusing on the effect of the personalities of men and officers on the development and fate of each mounted service.

Bruce Catton, *Mr. Lincoln's Army.* Garden City, NY: Doubleday, 1951. The first volume of this important and thorough three-volume history of the Army of the Potomac, describing the unit's formation and first engagements under General George McClellan.

——, *This Hallowed Ground: The Story of the Union Side of the Civil War.* New York: Doubleday, 1956. A good, readable, short history of the Civil War, written by one of the foremost authorities on the period.

Jack Coggins, *Arms and Equipment of the Civil War.* New York: Fairfax Press, 1962. Provides good, detailed information on Union and Confederate weapons, uniforms, and equipment; also explains the organization and duties of the infantry, cavalry, signal corps, corps of engineers, and so on. The text is highlighted by the author's vivid and historically accurate illustrations.

Henry Steele Commager, ed., *The Blue and the Gray: Two Volumes in One: The Story of the Civil War as Told by Participants.* New York: Fairfax Press, 1960. This excellent collection of original writings from the Civil War, complete with illustrations, is divided into sections covering enlistment, camp life, Civil War songs, prisons, important campaigns and battles, and other topics. There are several useful maps and a detailed bibliography.

Shelby Foote, *The Civil War: A Narrative.* 3 vols. New York: Vintage Books, 1958-1974. This scholarly work is a thorough and elegantly written military history of the Civil War. It covers in great detail and with considerable insight the ins and outs of the various campaigns, as well as the nature of the men who fought in them and the rigors and hardships they endured.

Philip Katcher, *The Army of Robert E. Lee.* London: Arms and Armour, 1994. A useful study of all aspects of the Army of Northern Virginia. Included are biographies of Lee and his generals and sketches of Confederate soldiers. Detailed information on each branch of service is rounded out by a discussion of how the army functioned as a whole in combat. A time line, orders of battle, and a bibliography supplement the text.

————, *The Civil War Source Book.* New York: Facts On File, 1992. Ten sections and several hundred entries furnish worthwhile information on the Union and Confederate armies. Topics include uniforms, weapons, camp life, discipline, prisons, battlefield medicine, and even salaries, to name a few. Also included are biographies of major figures, photographs, maps, a glossary, and a bibliography.

David Knapp Jr., *The Confederate Horsemen.* New York: Vantage Press, 1966. Informative biographical sketches of more than forty Confederate cavalry leaders.

Francis A. Lord, *They Fought for the Union.* Harrisburg, PA: Stackpole, 1960. An extremely thorough description of the Union army, its uniforms, insignia, weapons, and equipment. Quotes extensively from U.S. Army manuals and other documents, and provides photographs, drawings, and a very large bibliography.

James M. McPherson, *Battle Cry of Freedom: The Civil War Era.* Oxford: Oxford University Press, 1988. A very good one-volume history of the Civil War by a prominent historian of the period. Generous use of quotations and a good bibliography strengthen the text.

James M. McPherson, ed., *The Atlas of the Civil War.* New York: Macmillan, 1994. An excellent resource that is filled with good, large maps in color and well-reproduced black-and-white photographs from the Civil War. Informative essays accompany the maps, as well as review the happenings during each year of the Civil War. There is also a selected bibliography.

William J. Miller, *The Training of an Army: Camp Curtin and the North's Civil War.* Shippensburg, PA: White Mane, 1990. This history of one of the largest of the North's training camps presents a detailed picture of Civil War military instruction.

Stephen B. Oates, *Confederate Cavalry West of the River.* Austin: University of Texas Press, 1961. An interesting and informative account of the recruiting, equipping, and fielding of Confederate cavalry west of the Mississippi River.

James I. Robertson Jr., *Soldiers Blue and Gray.* Columbia: University of South Carolina Press, 1988. A very readable account of Federal and Confederate military life; firsthand accounts of enlistment, training, camp life, and battle are used to great effect.

Fred Albert Shannon, *The Organization and Administration of the Union Army 1861–1865*. 2 vols. Gloucester, MA: Peter Smith, 1965. A sound survey of all aspects of the Union army, filled with information about feeding and clothing volunteers, the evolution of discipline, and the daily life of the soldier.

Stewart Sifakis, *Who Was Who in the Civil War*. New York: Facts On File, 1988. Provides much interesting and worthwhile information on some 2,500 individuals who served the Union or the Confederacy. A time line, along with illustrations and photographs, enriches the text.

Stephen Z. Starr, *The Union Cavalry in the Civil War*. 3 vols. Baton Rouge: Louisiana State University Press, 1979. An impressively thorough history of the formation and evolution of the Union cavalry. Every aspect of cavalry life, from training to strategy to battle, is covered.

Richard Wheeler, ed., *Voices of the Civil War*. New York: Crowell, 1976. A good sampling of original writings from the Civil War. The selections are divided by campaign and battle and are accompanied by a time line and a bibliography.

Bell Irvin Wiley, *The Life of Billy Yank: The Common Soldier of the Union*. Indianapolis: Bobbs-Merrill, 1952.

————, *The Life of Johnny Reb: The Common Soldier of the Confederacy*. Indianapolis: Bobbs-Merrill, 1943. Two classic studies presenting in complete detail, often in the words of the participants, the life of the Union and Confederate soldier from enlistment to war's end. No better secondary sources exist for getting a feel for what it was like to soldier in the Civil War.

————, *They Who Fought Here*. New York: Macmillan, 1959. A good study of all aspects of the military life, North and South. Abundant period photographs supplement the text.

Frank Wilkeson, *Turned Inside Out: Recollections of a Private Soldier in the Army of the Potomac*. Lincoln: University of Nebraska Press, 1886. A graphic, vivid, and gripping account of enlistment and service in the Federal army during the last two years of the war.

★ Index ★

★ Picture Credits ★

Cover photo: Corbis Digital Stock

Corbis, 39 (top), 49, 50, 51, 60, 76, 77, 82, 90 (top), 94

Corbis Digital Stock, 10, 14, 30, 37, 41, 46, 55, 58, 64, 66, 84, 87, 90 (bottom, both), 91, 93

Corbis-Bettmann, 54

Dover Publications, Incorporated, 53, 56, 67

Library of Congress, 7, 9, 11, 15, 23, 24, 27 (bottom), 38, 39 (bottom), 69 (both), 71, 72, 78 (top), 80, 88, 89

Medford Historical Society Collection/Corbis, 27 (top), 28, 75

The Metropolitan Museum of Art, Gift of Mr. and Mrs. Jerry D. Berger, 1985, 34

National Archives, 33, 43, 48

North Wind Picture Archives, 13, 20, 22

Prints Old & Rare, 19

Lee Snider/Corbis, 25

Joseph Sohm; ChromoSohm, Inc./Corbis, 32

★ About the Author ★

James A. Corrick has been a professional writer and editor for twenty years and is the author of twenty books, as well as two hundred articles and short stories. His books *The Early Middle Ages, The Late Middle Ages, The Battle of Gettysburg, The Byzantine Empire, The Renaissance,* and *The Industrial Revolution* have been published by Lucent. Along with a Ph.D. in English, Corrick's academic background includes a graduate degree in the biological sciences. He has taught English, tutored minority students, edited magazines for the National Space Society, been a science writer for the Muscular Dystrophy Association, and edited and indexed books on history, economics, and literature for Columbia University Press, MIT Press, and others. He and his wife live in Tucson, Arizona; and when not writing, he reads, swims, walks, frequents bookstores, and holds forth on any number of topics. He is a member of the Arizona Historical Society and the Tucson Book Publishing Association.